BELIEF & UNBELIEF

BARBARA G. WALKER

Humanist Press
Washington, DC

BELIEF & UNBELIEF

BARBARA G. WALKER

HUMANIST PRESS

WASHINGTON, DC

Copyright © 2014 by Barbara G. Walker

Humanist Press
1777 T Street NW
Washington, DC, 20009
(202) 238-9088

www.humanistpress.com

All rights reserved. No part of this book may be reproduced in whole or in part without written permission from the publisher, except in the case of brief quotations embodied in critical articles and reviews; nor may any part of this book be reprinted or reproduced or utilized in any form or by any electronic, mechanical, or other means, now known or hereafter invented, including photocopying and recording, or in any information storage or retrieval system, without written permission from Humanist Press, LLC.

Printed book ISBN: 9780931779565
Ebook ISBN: 9780931779572

Cover design: Lisa Zangerl
Cover photo: © Rui Vale De Sousa | Dreamstime.com

Table of Contents

Works By Barbara G. Walker	1
Believing the Unbelievable	3
Does Religion Make People Good?	12
Bible Morality(King James Original)	23
God The Monster	34
Before Patriarchy	37
The Three Ages Of Woman	45
The Star In The East	60
What Is A Soul?	63
Cannibalism	68
Gnosticism: A Short History	71
Religion As The Root Of Sexism	81
The Islamic Holocaust	87
A Learning Experience	95
How Did Funerals Begin?	101
Religion And War	109
Animalia	122
Encountering The New Age	126
Atlantis: The Evolution Of A Myth	134
A Conversational Interview	141
Beauty	147
Women And War	153
Family And The Future	156
Recommended Reading	165
Bibliography	171
About The Author	177

Works By
BARBARA G. WALKER

GRAPHICS

The Barbara Walker Tarot Deck
The I Ching of the Goddess card deck

HISTORY/SPIRITUALITY

The Woman's Encyclopedia of Myths and Secrets
The Woman's Dictionary of Symbols and Sacred Objects
The Secrets of the Tarot: Origins, History, and Symbolism
The Essential Handbook of Women's Spirituality and Ritual
The Crone: Woman of Age, Wisdom and Power
The I Ching of the Goddess
The Book of Sacred Stones: Fact and Fallacy
in the Crystal World
The Skeptical Feminist: Discovering the Virgin,
Mother, and Crone
Restoring the Goddess: Equal Rites for Modern Women
Amazon: A Novel
Feminist Fairy Tales
Man Made God: A Collection of Essays

KNITTING AND KNITWEAR DESIGN

A Treasury of Knitting Patterns
A Second Treasury of Knitting Patterns
A Third Treasury of Knitting Patterns
(Charted Knitting Designs)
A Fourth Treasury of Knitting Patterns (Sampler Knitting)
Knitting From the Top
Mosaic Knitting
Barbara Walker's Learn-To-Knit Afghan Book
The Craft of Lace Knitting
The Craft of Cable-Stitch Knitting
The Craft of Multicolor Knitting

BELIEVING THE UNBELIEVABLE

Why are human beings so frequently prone to believing the unbelievable, trusting the improbable, being convinced by the very eccentricity of the impossible? As a species, we seem to want marvels and miracles more than facts. This might account for the almost assured success of nearly every would-be cult leader, no matter how bizarre his or her program may be. In fact, the wilder the better. The likes of Joseph Smith, Charles Taze Russell, Mary Baker Eddy, L. Ron Hubbard, and even the notorious Jim Jones readily attracted believers—as shown by such notable successes as Mormonism, Jehovah's Witnesses, Christian Science, and Scientology. Jones's cult may have had a similar burgeoning if it had not unfortunately turned suicidal.

Religious assertions that would seem improbable even in the context of Grimm's fairy tales are confidently put forth as believable and routinely labeled miraculous. The Catholic Church actually has a set agenda for identifying what it calls "genuine" miracles, which all Catholics are called upon to believe without doubting.

Doubt, in fact, is often described as an evil, whereas unquestioning credulity is the virtue known as "faith." Mark Twain defined faith as believing what you know ain't so.[1] Millions of literal Bible believers allow themselves to be convinced that a man can live for three days in the stomach of a "great fish," or that city walls can be knocked down by blowing a ram's horn, or that all humanity incestuously descended from a single pair, or that representatives of every animal species were once crammed into a boat built by a single man, either by twos or by sevens, depending on which chapter of Genesis you read. Oddly enough, when the same or similar stories are found in writings older than the bible, they are simply regarded as myths, and not believable.

Sam Harris says: "While religious faith is the one species of human ignorance that will not admit of even the possibility of corrections, it is still sheltered from criticism in every corner of your culture. Forsaking all valid sources of information about this world (both spiritual and mundane), our religions have seized upon ancient taboos and prescientific fancies as though they held ultimate metaphysical significance."[2]

But those who insist on obedience to bible literalism must be consistent enough to insist on some rather drastic behaviors. For instance, they must kill all homosexuals, witches, adulterers, non-virginal brides, all people who work on the Sabbath, and any family member who doesn't worship Yahweh. Jesus tells them that they may keep slaves, and even beat them "with many stripes" (Luke 12:47). Jesus also tells them that a man wishing to be sure of getting into heaven must be not just circumcised but castrated; he must be made a eunuch "for the kingdom of heaven's sake" (Matthew 19:12).

Perhaps this particular promise comforted the thousands of castrati who sang the soprano parts in church choirs through the centuries, when the church ruled that female voices were too "impure" to be heard at mass.

However, by the fifth century the church had found Jesus's view of castration to be something less than popular, and so quietly ignored it. It has been a consistent church policy to ignore any of Jesus's teachings that will not advance church welfare, such as the statement that it is easier for a camel to get through a needle's eye than for a rich man to get into heaven. Of course the church has flourished throughout the centuries precisely by promising blessed immortality to the rich.

Churches tell people what to believe. Saint Ignatius Loyola wrote: "We should always be disposed to believe that which appears white is really black, if the hierarchy of the Church so decides."[3]

If the belief happens to conflict with scripture, it's usually the text that gets sidelined, erased, or reinterpreted. Dubious attitudes toward church edicts are almost always regarded as wicked, due to devilish influence. To grant the doubters any credence at all is so devoutly feared by the devout that, throughout history, defenders of any faith have been notoriously prone to attack dissenters with wars, crusades, pogroms, rape, murder, pillage, torture, and the stake.

According to Michael Onfray, "In science the church has always been wrong about everything: faced with an epistemological truth, it automatically persecutes the discoverer. The history of science's relationship with Christianity yields a prodigious abundance of blunders and stupidity. Between the church's rejection of the heliocentric hypothesis of antiquity and its contemporary condemnations of genetic laws ... centuries of wasted opportunities for humankind are heaped up."[4]

The violence inspired by religion has exceeded all other forms of human violence. Indeed, it is commonplace for a nation wishing to institute aggression against another nation to depend on religion to label the enemy an evil to be eradicated. Faith can always be trusted to inspire some humans to destroy large numbers of other humans.

Literal believers like to claim that having faith in their own tradition, however improbable or impossible it may be, constitutes the major element of morality. It is claimed that disbelief in religious fictions is the very essence of immorality; any disbeliever must be completely without a moral code. Consequently, gullibility is made to seem morally superior to skeptical demands for proof. This is one reason why religion and science are usually at odds with one another, and also why many people are so thoroughly practiced in believing that they are easily victimized by liars, scammers and charlatans of all kinds. Is a person who readily believes the unbelievable really morally superior, or is he just diddled by his own naiveté?

Nevertheless, credulity creates its own version of reality. Tertullian wrote that it was the very impossibility of the Christian legend that convinced him of its truth: "I believe because it is impossible."[5] Saint Augustine wrote: "Faith is to believe what we do not see; and the reward of this faith is to see what we believe." And it is true that perfectly sane people can often convince themselves that they see what doesn't exist in external reality, when faith tells them it must be there.

Visions are not uncommon. People have always been eager to court the visionary experience, through dreams, drugs, drunkenness, fasting, meditating, or a variety of ritualistic procedures, and to regard such experience as somehow a superior truth. But the visionary experience is available to almost anyone. One can see vivid visions while enduring a high fever, or just by not eating for a week or so. Hallucination and vision are basically one and the same. The well-known "vision quest" of Native American tradition usually consisted of a period of fasting until a vision was achieved, to serve as the individual's personal totem.[6] Medieval saints and ascetics had a plethora of visions, probably as a result of their constant fasting.

Anthropologists have noted that pre-civilized people generally describe a dream as a real experience. Australian aborigines, for example, were in the habit of talking of their dreams as regular, verifiable parts of their lives, which is why their autobiographies included so many "tall tales" that seemed most unlikely in real life. Similarly, South and Central American tribes presented dreams and drug-induced visions as true happenings.

Hardly more sophisticated were the views of medieval Europeans, who often believed dreams to be prophetic messages or visitations from God, Jesus, angels, demons, spirits of the dead, and so forth. Some in the modern world still cling to such views. Sigmund Freud put a lot of faith in dreams as symbolic revelations of the inner mind, and used dream analysis as an adjunct to psychiatric treatment. When people see things that aren't there, asleep or awake, we still tend to give it some kind of transcendent significance.

Skeptics as well as believers are quite capable of seeing visions. I have done so myself, not only when suffering from fever, but also at times when a mental picture suddenly assumed the appearance of external reality, without any particular stimulus. I personally regarded such occasions as a kind of entertainment, somehow provided by my mind's eye to my physical eye; but I understand quite well how vivid and realistic a vision can be, while it lasts, which usually isn't more than a few minutes.

Of course we are all capable of seeing faces and forms in natural objects such as trees, clouds, shadows and such. These are not visions, strictly speaking, but they do demonstrate how imaginative our visual sense can be. Sometimes people put so much trust in these imaginings that they manage to convince themselves of a kind of reality even there. So egotistical is the human psyche that it wants to attribute deep meaning to everything it experiences.

Certainly, it is our ability to imagine that gives us art, fiction, drama, poetry, and many other ways of entertaining ourselves, as well as the means of innovation, discovery, and learning. It also gives us the ability to fool ourselves. We can easily "perceive" connections and interpretations having no basis in reality. We can see, in our mind's eye, what has only been described, but never seen except in human-made art: dragons, fairies, ghosts, unicorns, elves, gnomes, vampires, gods and demons, UFOs and aliens, Eden and Shangri-La, paradise and hell. We have mental pictures of all these things, just as clear as those of our own past. Visual arts like painting, sculpture, movies, and television give us even more precise memories of the nonexistent.

Carl Sagan pointed out that: "Over the years, a profusion of credulous, uncritical TV series and 'specials'–on ESP, channeling, the Bermuda triangle, UFOs, ancient astronauts, Bigfoot, and the like–have been spawned ... You can see a thirst for wonder here untempered by even rudimentary scientific skepticism. Pretty much whatever anyone says on camera is true."[7]

It's hardly surprising then that human beings are capable of perceiving, and believing in, that which has no existence except within the mind. We are taught as children that Santa Claus, the Easter Bunny, and the Tooth Fairy are real, then later we are told otherwise. But some beliefs, notably those of religion, are expected to remain through adulthood, and we may be accused of immorality if we abandon them.

There are beliefs that give us the comforting illusion of greater control over our own fate than we actually have. For many, religion does this; so do spiritualism, astrology, palmistry, divination, soothsaying, rune casting, clairvoyance, theosophy, crystal healing, card reading, good-luck charms, and hundreds of other so-called fringe beliefs. Miracle mongers, psychics, and seers of every stripe abound in our society, in many cases cynically exploiting the credulity of the masses, to make themselves a good living from their gullible followers, just as leaders of religious cults have done for countless ages.

What is it, then, that makes us so prone to believe the unbelievable, without demanding any reliable evidence?

One physiological fact applicable to all mammals is that they are born needing instruction in how to live. Most non-mammalian creatures—insects, reptiles, fish, etc.—are born with all their instincts innate, knowing how to conduct their lives without ever being shown a model. But infant mammals lack such complete instinctual patterns. They need an authority to care for them and teach them.

Complex social mammals, such as primates, learn from their mothers at first and then from other authority figures in their adulthood. They require some entity to tell them what to do, which may be why so many humans need to believe in some transcendent lawgiving power to obey, and why most of them are willing to subordinate their own desires to such real or imagined authority figures as gods, priests, governments, and military leaders. Their need to obey is so strong that sometimes it can even overcome the impulse for self-preservation and result in a voluntary sacrifice of life when so commanded.

This explains, too, why the original worldwide creation deities were Mother Goddesses, who were gradually replaced by paternal gods when humans discovered that men also had something to do with producing new lives. Since fatherhood was not obvious to primitive humans, any more than it is obvious to monkeys or whales or wolves, the mother was the nucleus of all early tribes and the first envisioned lawgiver. Many studies have shown how patriarchal societies tended to become more demanding and more violent than the matriarchies that preceded them. But always the deities, whether male or female, were envisioned as parents–today just as much as a million years ago.

When the growing individual realizes that human parents are fallible after all, the culture supplies an alternative in the imaginary parent who can do no wrong, and knows everything, and distributes transcendent rewards and punishments. Priesthoods and governments profit enormously from this, and so vigorously insist on preserving it, with all its rules and rituals, forever. Thus the effort continues always to clothe the imaginary parent figure in trappings of reality and to insist on faithful belief in the unbelievable. The adult's inner child takes comfort in such pseudo-parental visionings and seeks to maintain them, in fearful renunciation of any hint of doubt. You don't mess with a father who can have you tortured for all eternity.

This may be one reason why so many of us never seem to outgrow our naïve belief in the literal words of so-called holy scriptures, even though they have already been frequently altered by successive translations and editorializing, or when they are obviously absurd, impossible, or self-contradictory. Those who take the Old Testament literally have many such problems, including God's orders to kill homosexuals, witches, people who work on the Sabbath, and one's own family members who stray toward other gods (Deut. 13:6-9), and even the necessity to believe that the earth is only 6,000 years old.

One of the perennial excuses put forward by the modern believer is that there must be "reasons" for everything that happens, although we are not able to understand them. Therefore, some greater entity must exist who does understand them. "If there is no God, why is there a universe?" they ask, imagining that this question makes sense. But why should a universe demand a God? It is human egotism, again, that believes nothing can exist unless a human-type (but better) intelligence has somehow invented it.

Religion is sometimes put forward as a search for meaning, or even a discovery of meaning, even though what it really means is never stated. Actually, the "meaning of life" is different for every individual, and pinning the name of God on whatever is unknown can never make it any better known. Humans, the makers of language, like to make things seem real by giving them names. But in fact, using the name of God as a synonym for the unknown describes nothing, reveals nothing, and satisfies no real curiosity. Better to call it simply "the unknown" and let it go, hoping that science will continue to shed more and more light on our world in due time. What does it all mean? What does it have to mean? Can it not simply be, which is indeed what our perception shows?

The unknown may never be known, but that is no reason to afflict the human mind with absurd beliefs that must be affirmed, on pain of death or damnation or persecution, regardless of their total lack of evidence. As Dennet says, "Philosophy is questions that may never be answered. Religion is answers that may never be questioned."[8]

Yes, our universe is mysterious. Yes, we will never understand everything we want to understand. Yes, our brains have built-in limitations restricting our ability to know. Perhaps in further tens of thousands of years we can evolve into more intelligent beings.

We have dreams. We have visions. We have wishes and hopes. But let us not confuse them with the reality that surrounds us. We have a fascinating world to study and ponder; there is no need to misinterpret it for a specious comfort. Let us have done with unproven beliefs and unjustifiable faiths, and remain open to genuinely new knowledge. In the long run, that is what the human mind is all about.

Notes

1. Bufe, 182.
2. Harris, 223.
3. Bufe, 202.
4. Onfray, 83.
5. Smith, 227.
6. See http://www.ritesofpassagevisionquest.org/the-vision-quest.html.

7. Sagan, 374.
8. Dennet, 17.

DOES RELIGION MAKE PEOPLE GOOD?

The world has millions of kindly, generous, loving people who attribute their own good qualities to an abiding belief in a religion—usually one that features an equally kind and loving god. The world also has millions of kindly, generous, loving people who reject religion because they find a god either insufficiently loving or insufficiently credible. Each side may be more or less tolerant of the other, believers perhaps less so because many fear the wrath of their purportedly loving god if they should seem too soft-hearted toward his alleged enemies. Sometimes God seems not quite as forgiving as advertised.

Believers often assume that theirs is the majority opinion, but rarely know or care about theological particulars. Many don't care to examine their own beliefs, but follow their sect's rituals largely out of habit and social considerations, attending the same services as their friends and/or family, not because they have chosen them from the vast smorgasbord of available sects in any conscious or deliberate way, but just because it is their only experience.

The impression that people have to be religious in order to be good is earnestly promulgated by religious organizations, which have a vested interest in denying all evidence to the contrary. Fundamentalists like to define atheists as evil, or at least misguided. "I'll pray for you" says the condescending believer to the nonbeliever, thus reinforcing his own opinion that God will listen to him and do as he directs. One of the most revered tenets of belief is that God may be petitioned and will alter his behavior accordingly. How gratifying, to imagine that God will change his intentions in obedience to one's request! Surely, belief in the effective power of prayer is the ultimate ego trip for its practitioner. Even as grownups, childlike people imagine that there is a Parent who will pay attention to their wants.

But is it really true that religion makes people more kindly, generous or loving? History tends to disprove this. The worst wars, the most vicious Inquisitions, the cruelest pogroms and persecutions were both fomented and supported by religion. Soldiers and crusaders have always been taught that the enemy consists of people who lack the true faith, and so deserve to be massacred. The biblical God who supposedly said "Thou shalt not kill" ordered hundreds of genocidal slaughters and summary executions (including the blood sacrifice of his allegedly beloved son). Wars are seldom perpetrated without the support of religious authorities. Chaplains are even made handy to the battlefield, to assure soldiers that God says they shalt kill as many of the enemy as possible.

As a means of motivating people to be cruel or inhumane, there is no more potent force than religion. Men of patriarchal cultures have been committing heinous acts in the name of their God ever since they created a god for themselves. It seems that the earlier, Goddess-oriented, nature-centered religions were far less cruel.

From the slaughters recorded in the Bible, early Christians' butchery of European pagans, the "holy" Crusades, and later European Christians' genocide of New World natives, to the twentieth-century holocaust in Nazi Germany, religion has been a major rationale for every kind of inhumanity. It has been the cause of the monstrous two-millennium abuse of women on the specious ground of a mythic original sin committed by Eve, and of preposterous witch hunts of the Inquisition. Though estimates of the death toll vary widely, there is no denying that much killing can be done by an organization that lasted over 500 years and covered much of Europe, with legal confiscation of the victims' property as its primary encouragement.

Since St. Augustine announced that Eve–and hence collective woman–was responsible for original sin, rabid sexism has been a major pillar of patriarchal religious tradition.[1] Clement of Alexandria said every woman should be ashamed of being female. According to the Gospel of Thomas, Saint Peter said that women are not worthy of life.[2] St. Thomas Aquinas said every woman is born defective, lower than a slave, only meant by God to be "in subjection" to her husband.[3] A nineteenth-century Anglican churchman wrote that a woman is "intrinsically inferior in excellence, imbecile by sex and nature, weak in body, inconstant in mind, and imperfect and infirm in character."[4] In the 1890s the president of a leading theological seminary noted that the Bible commands "the subjection of women forever."[5] Orestes Brownson said a woman must be under male control, otherwise she is "out of her element and a social anomaly, sometimes a hideous monster, which men seldom are, excepting through a woman's influence."[6] The holy father John Scotus Erigena wrote that when the heavens finally open in glory, women will be eliminated, because God embodied the sinless part of humanity in men and the sinful part in women.[7] According to the official handbook of the Inquisition, the *Malleus Maleficarum* (A Hammer for Witches), "all wickedness is but little to the wickedness of a woman."[8] Even the twentieth-century *Catholic Encyclopedia* asserts that the female sex is inferior to the male sex in both body and soul.[9]

Marriage to a woman was not recommended by early Christian fathers. St. Ambrose called marriage a crime against God.[10] Tatian called marriage "a polluted and foul way of life."[11] According to Origen, matrimony is impure and unholy; and according to St. Jerome, the purpose of every godly man should be "to cut down with the ax of Virginity the wood of Marriage."[12] Tertullian called marriage a moral crime, "more dreadful than any punishment or any death."[13] St. Bernard opined that it is easier to bring the dead back to life than for a man to live with a woman without endangering his own soul.[14] For the first half of the Christian era, marriage was a civil ceremony only, having nothing to do with religion. It was not until the Council of Trent in 1538 that a Christian ceremony was considered essential to a valid marriage.[15] "Nothing is further from the truth than the contention of modern divines that the Church from the first patronized and sanctified an institution which was in reality only imposed on her... Nothing is more remarkable than the tardiness with which liturgical forms for the marriage ceremony were evolved in the Church."[16] Eventually, it seems, the church realized that there was an additional source of income to be exploited.

Marriage finally became acceptable to the churches when laws were established that could make it a means of depriving women of incomes and property, and making wives the equivalent of slaves. Some of the eastern churches made it a wedding custom for a bride to kneel and place her bridegroom's foot on her head, and accept a stroke from a fancy ceremonial whip. Wife-beating was so routine in Christian countries that the Alsatian decorative symbol for "marriage" was a toy man beating a toy wife. Martin Luther thought himself a very lenient husband because he didn't beat his wife with a stick, but only punched her in the head to prevent her from "getting saucy."[17] In Victorian times, Blackstone's legal "rule of thumb" decreed that a man could beat his wife with a stick as long as it was no thicker than his thumb, "in order to enforce the salutary restraints of domestic discipline." Up to the nineteenth century, British law allowed acts of assault to be legally innocent if committed by a husband against a wife.[18] Apparently, however, beatings with clubs thicker than the thumb had been shown to result in broken bones that tended to interfere with wives' getting their work done. Only in the last century did most Christian countries finally get around to declaring wife-beating a crime, though it is still acceptable under Islam.

A slave may be defined as a person who is forced to work, but receives no payment other than food, shelter and clothing; who is expected to be obedient, and may be beaten or otherwise abused at the discretion of the master; who is legally immobilized and considered to be property. Under patriarchal religion, this definition applied equally to a wife. In addition, female slaves were freely used as sexual objects by their masters and forced to bear the master's offspring. This equally applies to wives under a religious system that denies them access to birth control or abortion.

Religion not only taught men that they may enslave women with God's blessing; it also taught many people to believe that they are God's chosen ones, greatly superior to those of other colors or other beliefs; therefore the latter may be enslaved or slaughtered, also with God's blessing. Again and again the biblical God recommends huge slaughters of such people; and "thine eye shall have no pity on them" (Deut. 7:16). Prejudicial traces of such ideas are still common today. Religion does not necessarily promote love for humanity in general.

According to the recent Baptist Faith and Message, Article 18, of the Southern Baptist Convention, "A wife is to submit graciously to the servant leadership of her husband." One minister explained to a sociologist: "Wife beating is on the rise because men are no longer leaders in their homes. I tell women they must go back home and be more submissive." One battered woman was told by her pastor: "No matter what he is doing to you, he is still your spiritual head ... Remember, no matter what, you owe it to him and to God to live in submission to your husband. You'll never be happy until you submit to him."[19]

The duality implicit in god-and-devil, heaven-and-hell, good-and-evil leads to a kind of elitism that assures the believer of his own superiority and the general unworthiness of The Other. Religion greatly enhances the We/They syndrome. One's own group is destined for eternal bliss, while the outsiders merit eternal agony–which has been exhaustively and very graphically described, although the bliss remains undefined.

The strangest thing about the notion of eternal bliss is that it is not clearly envisioned. There may be vague references to the joy of spending all eternity singing the praises of an incredibly vain and praise-hungry God. But after an hour or two of that, might not one become bored and wish to move on to some other entertainment? If there is no other entertainment, to spend all the rest of eternity doing nothing but singing God's praises may sound less like heaven and more like hell. David Lloyd George, British Prime Minister from 1916 to 1922, said the idea of heaven frightened him more than hell: "I pictured heaven as a place where there would be perpetual Sundays ... from which there would be no escape ... It was a horrible nightmare. The conventional Heaven with its angels perpetually singing nearly drove me mad in my youth and made me an atheist."[20]

The idea put forth by several ancient pagan societies, that paradise involves an eternal orgasm, was soon shot down by sex-phobic patriarchies even though some traces still exist in the Muslim concept of the post-mortem *houris* for male heroes, though of course women have no comparable angelic lovers. Usually, patriarchal religions have seriously distrusted sensual pleasures because of their association with femaleness. Western attitudes toward sexuality have suffered many poisonous suppressions and misinterpretations as a result. Over the centuries, religion seems to have generated more hatred than love, and more war than peace.

We might wonder, then: are people good because of religion, or in spite of it? Is it religiously-generated fear that keeps most people from harming others, or is it simply a natural respect for one's fellow beings, such as demonstrated all the time by animals? Do people really need the paranoia generated by horrendous descriptions of the tortures awaiting them in hell, in order to treat their fellow human beings decently? Or might these dreadful if imaginary fears tend to make people behave more cruelly toward others?

Indeed, Christianity's idea of hell seems to have inspired a truly horrifying degree of sadism in its adherents, as shown by the incredible tortures routinely used by the Inquisition and other Christian authorities. Even revered church Fathers showed a certain repellent lip-licking anticipation when they envisioned the agonies of hell. Tertullian wrote, "How I shall laugh and be glad and exult when I see these wise philosophers, who teach that the gods are indifferent and men soulless, roasting and browning before their own disciples in hell."[21] And the blessed St. Thomas Aquinas promised similar pleasures to all faithful Christians: "In order that the happiness of the saints may be more delightful and that they may give to God more copious thanks for it, they are permitted perfectly to behold the sufferings of the damned."[22] As Joseph McCabe remarked, "Any body of men who believe in hell will persecute whenever they have the power."[23]

Religion seems infinitely accommodating, in that its interpretations take the shape of whatever personality types are adopting it. Kindly people, raised by affectionate parents and taught altruistic values, embrace a religion of goodwill and view love as a primary virtue. Those who are harshly treated in childhood tend to become more rigid, righteous, and prone to worship a god who hates and punishes. Religious scriptures, notoriously self-contradictory, have plenty of sanctions for either point of view. The loving and forgiving God is just as conceivable as the wrathful, jealous, implacably punitive one. In condemning the cruelty of medieval and Renaissance Christianity we might do well to remember that "spare the rod and spoil the child" was the watchword of most families, and not only women but also children were routinely beaten for the slightest offenses.

So it may appear that culture shapes religion, rather than the other way around. Through the centuries up to modern times, the Bible has been extensively revised and reinterpreted to sweeten its nastier passages and give its God a better profile. The barbaric central idea of the bloodthirsty Father demanding the sacrifice of the blameless Son is still intrinsic to Christianity, but in time even that may be found unacceptable and "reinterpreted" into an altogether different scenario.

Religious people often protest that it is wrong to attack religion, because religion alone can make people virtuous. History shows that this is hardly the case. Every improvement in criminal law, every progress in social humaneness has been opposed by organized religion, just as much as our progress in scientific understanding of our world has been so opposed. It would seem that religion does not initiate moral virtue in the community, but rather grudgingly reflects it, once the community has sufficiently overcome religious objections to its progress and become somewhat more enlightened. We should remember that in our country, churches endorsed slavery, public hangings, flagellation, wife-beating, whipping of schoolchildren, and many other abuses.

Religion may pretend to be all things to all people, but it might be beneficial to consider its costs. Huge amounts of time, attention, and tax-free money are spent on religious trappings that might be better spent on improvement of living conditions for more people, or on genuine education rather than on mythical shadowlands. It is surely unfortunate that the religious imagination can so easily justify war, hatred and cruelty. H. L. Mencken once remarked: "The most common of all follies is to believe passionately in the palpably not true. It is the chief occupation of mankind." As Stephen Weinberg said: "With or without religion you would have good people doing good things and evil people doing evil things. But for good people to do evil things, that takes religion."[24]

What was arguably the greatest evil of the twentieth century was helped along by the Catholic Church, which "signed a concordat with Adolf Hitler as soon as the chancellor took office in 1933. The Catholic Church provided the Nazis with genealogical records ... supported, defended, and aided the pro-Nazi Ustachi regime in Croatia ... The Catholic Church, although fully aware of the policy of extermination set in motion in 1942, did not condemn it in private or in public, and never ordered any priest or bishop to condemn the criminal regime in the hearing of his flock ... The Catholic Church, in the person of Cardinal Bertram, ordered a requiem mass in memory of Adolf Hitler. Even better, the Catholic Church did for the Nazis what it had never done for a single Jew: it set up a network designed to smuggle war criminals out of Europe. ... The Catholic Church promoted into its hierarchy people who had performed important tasks for the Hitler regime. And the Catholic Church will never apologize for any of these things."[25]

The greatest twentieth century war crime of the United States was solemnly blessed by Father George Zabelka as he called down God's benefice on the crew of the Enola Gay, as they were taking off to drop their atomic bomb on Hiroshima.[26] Upon hearing of the bomb's huge destruction of defenseless civilians, President Truman remarked, "This is the greatest thing in history."[27]

Does religion actually make people less violent? Not according to the statistics. The U.S. has been termed the most religious of all industrialized nations, but its murder rate is five times that of Sweden, six times that of Britain, seven times that of Japan. Louisiana has the highest churchgoing rate in the country, and a murder rate more than twice the national average.[28]

Richard Dawkins summed up the problem of religious intolerance:

> Even if religion did no other harm in itself, its wanton and carefully nurtured divisiveness ... would be enough to make it a significant force for evil in the world.[29]

John Lash points out that: "History shows that the religious ideals attached to the salvation narrative have consistently been used to legitimate violence, rape, genocide, and destruction of the natural world ... Good and decent Muslims and their Christian and Jewish counterparts stand aside, watching what is done in the name of their cherished beliefs ... The people who commit and promote violence and murder in the expression of religious belief may be a minute fraction of the faithful, but they are the ones who determine the course of events, shape history, affect society, and threaten the biosphere ... Religion claims to make the world safe, but the right future for humanity may depend on making the world safe from religion."[30]

And Michael Onfray adds: "From the earliest texts of the Old Testament to the present day, the assertion of one God, violent, jealous, quarrelsome, intolerant, and bellicose, has generated more hate, bloodshed, deaths, and brutality than it has peace. ... It justifies the Crusades, the Inquisition, the French religious wars, massacres, the stake, the Index.... North American ethnocides, support for twentith-century fascist movements, and the centuries-long temporal hold of the Vatican over the smallest details of daily life."[31]

In an article published in *Free Inquiry*, Aug./Sept. 2012, P. Z. Myers writes:

> Religion is ridiculous and corrupt. Beyond the concept of a god, the institutions supporting god-belief seem to be imploding in embarrassing ways. The Catholic Church has been exposed as a monstrous organ of depravity that cultivates child rapists. The Protestants have splintered into a

thousand sects, most of which seem Elmer Gantryish, dedicated to fleecing the flock and reinforcing their own privileges. Islam spends its time trying to wind the clock back to medieval ignorance, trying to prove that it can be more barbarous than the West, then lashing out violently every time someone points out that it has a habit of lashing out violently.

As children naturally outgrow Santa Claus, the tooth fairy, and the ogre under the bed, so humanity in general may need to outgrow its gods and devils. Our collective imagination could be much better employed, in finding ways to understand our world more clearly, to help rather than harm, and to halt the runaway overpopulation with which we threaten the life of our planet, and of course, of ourselves as well.

Notes

1. Lederer, 162.
2. Malvern, 1.
3. de Riencourt, 219.
4. Bullough, 98, 187, 203.
5. Stanton, 194.
6. Bullough, 309.
7. de Riencourt, 227.
8. Kramer & Sprenger, 44.
9. Catholic Encyclopedia, "Woman." http://www.newadvent.org/cathen/15687b.htm.
10. Briffault 3, 373.
11. Bullough, 113.
12. Fielding, 82, 114.
13. Lederer, 163.
14. Campbell, M.I. 95.
15. Eisenach, 54.
16. Briffault 3, 248.
17. Davidson, 100.
18. Langley & Levy, 34-36.

19. Blaker, 91-93.
20. Cranston, 335.
21. Bufe, 217.
22. *Ibid.*, 215.
23. *Ibid.*, 217.
24. Konner, 30.
25. Onfray, 185.
26. *Ibid.*, 192.
27. Condren, 202.
28. Blaker, 136.
29. Dawkins, 262.
30. Lash, 239, 266.
31. Onfray, 41-42.

BIBLE MORALITY
(King James Original)

---

1. KILLING. (As in "Thou shalt not"???)

The Biblical God personally kills a total of 371,186 people, not counting his slaughter of almost every living thing in Genesis 7. The Biblical God also orders the killing of a total of 1,862,265.

- Gen. 22:2 - God accepts human sacrifices, (including that of Jesus, later); he demands that Isaac become one.
- Ex. 12:29 - God kills all the Egyptians' firstborn children.
- Ex. 15:3 - God is a god of war.
- Ex. 21:15-17 - Anyone who strikes or curses a parent must be killed.
- Ex. 22:18 - Every witch must be killed.
- Ex. 22:19-20 - You must kill anyone who "lieth with a beast," or who sacrifices to any god other than Yahweh.
- Ex. 31:15 - Anyone who works on the Sabbath must be killed.
- Lev. 20:10,13, 27 - You must kill adulterers, homosexuals, wizards, and spirit mediums.
- Lev. 21:9 - Any priest's daughter who fornicates must be burned alive.
- Lev. 24:16 - Blasphemers must be killed.
- Num. 16:27-33 - God caused the whole tribe of Korah—men, women, and children—to be buried alive.
- Num. 21:3 - God caused the destruction of all the Canaanites.
- Deut. 3:4-6 - God is pleased that his warriors destroyed 60 cities and all their inhabitants.
- Deut. 7:16 - You must kill all the people God delivers into your hands, and "thine eye shall have no pity upon them."
- Deut. 13:5 - Any prophet or "dreamer of dreams," who serves another god, must be killed.
- Deut. 13:6-9 - If your brother, son, daughter, wife, or friend

tempts you to worship other gods, "thou shalt surely kill him."

Deut. 13:13-15 - If the people of any city worship other gods, you must slaughter them all, including their cattle.

Deut. 17:2-5 - Any man or woman who worships other deities of sun, moon, or stars must be stoned to death.

Deut. 18:20 - False prophets must be killed.

Deut. 20:16-17 - God commands complete destruction of all Hittites, Amorites, Canaanites, Perizzites, Hivites, and Jebusites, and "thou shalt save alive nothing that breatheth."

Deut. 22:13-21 - A bride found not to be a virgin must be stoned to death.

Deut. 22:22 - Adulterers must be killed.

Deut. 22:23-24 - A betrothed virgin girl who is raped within city limits, and fails to cry out, must be killed along with her rapist.

Deut. 28:15-27 - If you don't obey God's commandments, he will punish you with consumption, fever, extreme burning, blasting, mildew, hemorrhoids, the scab, the itch, the botch of Egypt, etc., etc.

Josh. 6:1-21 - God's warriors destroyed Jericho and killed every man, woman, child, and domestic animal.

Josh. 8:25 - God's warriors killed 12,000 people in the city of Ai.

Josh. 19:47 - The children of Dan wanted more room, so they "smote" the population of Leshen and took their territory.

Judges 1:17,18 - Judah and Simeon "slew the Canaanites" who inhabited Zephath, Gaza, Askelon and Ekron.

Judges 11:30-39 - In accord with a promise to God, Jephthah was forced to burn his virgin daughter to death as a sacrifice.

Judges 15:15 - A godly miracle, apparently, enables Samson to kill 1,000 men with the jawbone of an ass.

Judges 20:46-48 - At Gibeah, Benjamin's men killed 25,000 people and burned every town.

1 Sam. 6:19 - God kills 50,070 people for trying to peek into the Ark.

1 Sam. 15:3 - God commands the destruction of Amalek: "Slay both men and women, infant and suckling, ox and sheep, camel and ass."

2 Sam. 6:6-7 - God kills Uzzah for touching the Ark, even though he was trying to save it from falling off its oxcart.

1 Kings 18:40 - God commands the slaughter of "prophets of Baal."

1 Kings 20:35-36 - Because a man didn't "obey the voice of the Lord," a lion was sent to kill him.

2 Kings 2:23-24 - God sent bears to tear apart 42 children for making fun of Elisha's bald head.

2 Kings 10:23-25 - God commands the killing of a multitude in the temple of Baal.

2 Kings 19:35 - God's angel killed 185,000 Assyrians in a single night.

1 Chron. 21:14 - God kills 70,000 Israelites with a pestilence.

2 Chron. 15:13 - Any man or woman who refuses to "seek the Lord God of Israel" must be killed.

Job 1 - God arranges the killing of Job's children, servants, and animals.

Isa. 13:16 - God promises that all the Babylonians' children will be "dashed to pieces before their eyes"; their wives will be raped.

Isa. 45:7 - God says "I create evil."

Jer. 48:10 - Killing for God is mandatory; God curses anyone who "keepeth back his sword from blood."

Jer. 50:21 - God commands that the people of Merathaim and Pekod be "utterly destroyed."

Ezek. 9:5-7 - God calls for purging in Jerusalem: "let not your eye spare, neither have ye pity: slay utterly old and young, both maids and little children, and women ... fill the courts with the slain."

Ezek. 35:8 - God promises to fill the mountains, hills, valleys and rivers with slain men.

Hosea 13:16 - God promises to have Samarian infants dashed

to pieces, and pregnant women will have their bellies slashed open.

Nahum 1:2 - God is jealous, full of vengeance and wrath.

Zeph. 1:3 - God threatens to destroy everything, man and beast, birds and fishes.

Zeph. 1:18 – "The whole land shall be devoured by the fire of his jealousy."

Zeph. 3:6 - God brags that he has destroyed many nations.

Zech. 13:3 - A false prophet must be killed by his father and mother.

2. RAPE

Ex. 21:7,8 - A father may sell his daughter to be a "maidservant" (or sex slave) who must "please her master."

Num. 31:18 - God orders his warriors to kill every living thing in each captured city, except the virgin girls, who are to be raped and turned into sex slaves. According to verse 35, there were 32,000 virgin girls thus taken.

Deut. 21:11-12 - If a warrior likes the look of a female war captive, he can take her to be one of his "wives."

Deut. 22:28-29 - A man who rapes a virgin may take her for a wife if he pays her father 50 shekels of silver. (Yet a bride found not to be a virgin must be killed - Deut. 22:24).

Judges 5:30 - The spoils of war include "a damsel or two" for every man.

Judges 21:12-21 - God's warriors killed all the inhabitants of Jabesh-gilead except for 400 virgin girls, who were taken as slaves. If there are not enough girls to go around, God's warriors may raid neighboring towns for more to rape.

3. SLAVERY

Gen. 9:25 - God cursed the son of Ham, who was the son of Noah, with perpetual slavery for the crime of seeing his father naked. (Ham was formerly considered the ancestor of all Negroes.)

Ex. 21:2-4 - A Hebrew male slave may marry and have children, and may go free after six years; but his family remains the property (or hostages?) of his master.

Ex. 21:7 - A man may sell his daughter as a sex slave.

Ex. 21:20-21 - A man may be punished for beating a male or female slave to death, but if the victim survives the beating for a few days, then there is no penalty.

Lev. 19:20 - When a man has sex with a female slave (or "bondmaid") who is betrothed, she must be scourged.

Eph. 6:5 - Paul says slaves must obey their masters "with fear and trembling."

Titus 2:9 - Paul says slaves must obey and please their masters.

1 Tim. 6:1 - Paul says slaves must "count their masters worthy of all honor."

4. CANNIBALIZING CHILDREN

Deut. 28:53 - Among the curses God threatens: "Thou shalt eat the fruit of thine own body, the flesh of thy sons and of thy daughters."

Jer. 19:8-9 - God threatens to make Jerusalem desolate, and to make its people "eat the flesh of their sons and the flesh of their daughters."

Ezek. 5:10 - Because the people have not kept his statutes, God promises that "the fathers shall eat the sons, and the sons shall eat the fathers."

5. WAS JESUS ETHICAL?

Matt. 5:28-32 - Jesus says marriage to a divorcee is adultery; and a man who ogles a woman has already committed adultery; and that you must cut off your hand or pluck out your eye if it offends.

Matt. 6:19,34 - Jesus says don't save any money, and don't plan ahead.

Matt. 8:32 - Having no regard for private property, Jesus causes the destruction of a herd of someone else's pigs.

Matt. 10:34 - Jesus says he brings not peace on earth, but "a sword."

Matt. 19:12 - Jesus condones castration.

Mark 11:13 - Jesus condemns a fig tree for not bearing figs out of season.

Mark 14:4-7 - Jesus says it is more important to anoint him with precious ointment than to give to the poor.

Mark 16:18 - Jesus says anyone who believes in him can play with venomous snakes or drink poison without harm. (This has been often tried, with rather unsatisfactory results.)

Luke 12:47-48 - Jesus says it is permissible to whip slaves.

Luke 14:26 - Jesus says no man can be his disciple unless he hates his parents, siblings, wife, children, and himself as well.

Luke 19:27 - Jesus explains by parable that anyone who denies his rulership must be killed.

John 15:6 - Jesus says anyone who doesn't believe in him must be burned.

Acts 5:5-10 - Ananias and his wife Sapphira were killed for withholding money from the church.

2 John 1:10-11 - A Christian is forbidden to offer hospitality to a non-Christian, not even to wish him "Godspeed" on parting.

6. WOMEN IN THE NEW TESTAMENT

1 Cor. 11:3-10 - Women are inferior "because man was not created for woman, but woman was created for man." Every woman "while praying or prophesying" must have her head covered "because of the angels," meaning the spirits (it used to be believed that women's hair attracts spirits).

1 Cor. 14:34-35 - Women must not speak in church; it is shameful. If they want to ask questions, they must ask their husbands at home.

Eph. 5:22 - Wives must submit to their husbands as they would to God.

1 Tim. 2:11-14 - A woman must not teach, or hold authority over a man, but must "learn in silence with all subjection"

because "Adam was not deceived, but the woman being deceived was in the transgression." (So, being gullible is the original sin.)

1 Tim. 5:9 - Paul says the only women acceptable by the council of elders are devout, monogamous women over the age of 60.

7. SILLINESS

Gen. 1:11-15 - God made all green plants on the third day of creation, but neglected to supply the sun (on which both plants and "days" depend) until the fourth day.

Gen. 6:6,7 - Because a few people displeased him, God "repented" having made the world, and decided to destroy all life on earth.

Gen. 7:2 - God tells Noah to populate the ark with "clean" (*i.e.*, edible) beasts by sevens, and with "unclean" or inedible beasts by twos. It has been calculated that if every species of land animal was represented, with food for all, including extra animals for the carnivores to eat, the ark would have to be about the size of the state of California.

Gen. 7:19-20 - The Flood covered "all the high hills that were under the whole heaven" and all the mountains were covered to a depth of 15 cubits, something in excess of 20 feet covering the summit of Mt. Everest: far too much water ever to drain.

Lev. 11:5-6 - God thinks hares are cud-chewing animals.

Deut. 22:5 - All cross-dressers, or women who wear pants, are "abominations."

Deut. 25:11,12 - A woman who seizes a man's genitals, even to defend her husband from an attacker, must have her hand cut off.

Deut. 33:17 - God believes in unicorns.

2 Kings 20:8-11 - At the request of King Hezekiah, God helped Isaiah make the sundial's shadow go backward.

Matt. 5:22 - Jesus says anyone who calls another "fool" will go to hell, but then he does it himself (Matt. 23:17).

1 Tim. 2:9 - Christian women are forbidden to braid their hair or wear jewelry.

James 5:14-15 - Prayer by the elders of the church is the only sure cure for sickness. (Christian Science, anyone?)

Which Ten Commandments do you prefer? Ex. 20, Ex. 34, Deut. 5, or Deut. 27?

8. BIBLE CONTRADICTIONS

Gen. 1:25-26 - God made all the animals before Adam.
Gen. 2:19 - God made Adam before all the animals.

Eph. 2:8-9 - "For by grace are ye saved through faith, and that not of yourselves... Not of works, lest any man should boast."
Jas. 2:24 – "By works a man is justified, and not by faith only."

Eccl. 9:5 - "The dead know not any thing; neither have they any more reward; for the memory of them is forgotten."
John 11:26 - Jesus says, "Whosoever liveth and believeth in me shall never die."

Luke 6:27 - "Love your enemies, do good to them which hate you."
Luke 19:27 - Jesus says, "Those mine enemies, which would not that I should reign over them, bring hither and slay them before me."

Judges 1:19 - God can't prevail against chariots of iron.
Matt. 19:26 - "With God all things are possible."

Num. 14:22 - God has been tempted ten times.
Jas. 1:13 - God can't be tempted.

Jer. 13:14 - God will not pity, nor spare, nor have mercy.
Jas. 5:11 - "The Lord is very pitiful, and of tender mercy."

Ex. 20:5 - God will punish descendants for their parents' sins

"unto the third and fourth generation."
Ezek. 18:20 - "The son shall not bear the iniquity of the father."

Prov. 3:13 - "Happy is the man that findeth wisdom, and the man that getteth understanding."
Eccl. 1:18 - "In much wisdom is much grief; and he that increaseth knowledge increaseth sorrow."

Matt. 27:34 - At the crucifixion, Jesus was given vinegar and gall.
Mark 15:23 - At the crucifixion, Jesus was given wine and myrrh (but did not drink it).

1 Sam. 8:2 - Samuel's firstborn son was named Joel.
1 Chron. 6:28 - Samuel's firstborn son was named Vashni.

Luke 20:35 - Jesus says that to be counted worthy of resurrection, one should remain unmarried.
1 Tim. 3:2,12 - Bishops and deacons should be husbands of one wife.

Eccl. 1:4 - "The earth abideth forever."
Matt. 24:35; Luke 21:33 – "Heaven and earth shall pass away."

Matt. 7:8 - "For every one that asketh receiveth; and he that seeketh findeth; and to him that knocketh it shall be opened."
Luke 13:24 - "Many, I say unto you, will seek to enter in, and shall not be able."

Acts 9:7 - Paul's companions heard a voice, but saw no man.
Acts 22:9 - Paul's companions saw a light, but heard no voice.

Matt. 27:5 - Judas hanged himself.
Acts 1:18 - Judas died of a fall, when he "burst asunder in the midst, and all his bowels gushed out."

COMMENTS ON THE BIBLE:

Thomas Paine: "It would be more consistent that we called it the word of a demon, than the word of God. It is a history of wickedness, that has served to corrupt and brutalize mankind; and, for my part, I sincerely detest it, as I detest everything that is cruel."[1]

Elizabeth Cady Stanton: "The Bible and Church have been the greatest stumbling blocks in the way of women's emancipation."[2]

Richard Dawkins: "The God of the Old Testament is arguably the most unpleasant character in all fiction. Jealous and proud of it, a petty, unjust, unforgiving control-freak; a vindictive, genocidal, filicidal, pestilential, megalomaniacal, sadomasochistic, capriciously malevolent bully. ... Those who wish to base their morality literally on the Bible have either not read it or not understood it."[3]

Robert Ingersoll: "If the devil had inspired a book, will some Christians tell us in what respect, on the subjects of slavery, polygamy, war and liberty, it would have differed from some parts of the Old Testament? ... How long, O how long will mankind worship a book? How long will they grovel in the dust before the ignorant legends of a barbaric past?"[4]

Thomas Jefferson: "The Christian God is a three-headed monster; cruel, vengeful and capricious... we discover [in the gospels] a groundwork of vulgar ignorance, of things impossible, of superstition, fanaticism and fabrication."[5]

Steven Pinker: "Aside from the approximately one thousand (biblical) verses in which Yahweh himself appears as the direct executioner of violent punishments, and the many texts in which the Lord delivers the criminal to the punisher's sword, in over one hundred other passages Yahweh expressly gives the command to kill people."[6]

Voltaire: "Christianity is the most ridiculous, absurd, and bloody religion that has ever infected the world."[7]

Isaac Asimov: "The Bible is the most potent force for atheism ever conceived."[8]

Ashley Montagu: "The Good Book—one of the most remarkable euphemisms ever coined."[9]

A.A. Milne: "The Old Testament is responsible for more atheism, agnosticism, disbelief–call it what you will–than any book ever written."[10]

Herbert J. Muller: "No educated Christian actually accepts the whole Bible as literally true. The most orthodox resorts to historical or metaphorical explanations as he deals with manifest inconsistencies, or explains away the plain meanings of such texts as 'Thou shalt not suffer a witch to live.' Indeed, the ministry could hardly survive without figurative interpretations; every Sunday thousands of sermons resound with meanings that the authors of the Bible could never have dreamed of."[11]

Matthew Tindal, 1730: "It's an odd jumble to prove the truth of a book by the truth of doctrines it contains, and at the same time conclude those doctrines to be true because contained in the book."[12]

The official Baptist "Faith and Message," 1989: "The Bible has God for its author, salvation for its end, and truth without any admixture of error, for its matter."

Notes

1. Bufe, 208.
2. *Ibid.*, 210.
3. Dawkins, 31, 237.
4. Bufe, 197-198.
5. *Ibid.*, 200.
6. Pinker, 10.
7. Stein, 715.
8. Mills, 27.
9. *Ibid.*, 53.
10. *Ibid.*, 54.
11. Muller, 91.
12. Stein, 238.

GOD THE MONSTER

In my childhood Sunday school, when I was shown a graphic picture of Jesus' execution scene, I cried. I wanted to know why all-powerful God couldn't protect his own son, of all people. Then I was told that Jesus' death was deliberately planned by God. I was shocked.

My tears were due not only to pity for the agony shown, but also to a horrified realization that God, who was said to be loving and all-forgiving, would not forgive human sins until his anger was appeased by this atrocious blood sacrifice of his allegedly beloved son.

What kind of a father was this? I wondered. Was he a God whom one could trust, or admire, or even like? If he was both kindly and all-powerful, why couldn't he just forgive everyone right off, without insisting on the brutal murder of his child? And why should such a murder appease him in the first place? Was God so sadistic as to demand bloodshed and pain for retribution?

It was a jarring moment. All my previous impressions were overturned, and I was forced to take a lonely excursion into the illogic of theology. I learned later that, in spite of the blood sacrifice that supposedly released humanity from an inevitable hell, people were still being sent to hell anyway—even good, innocent people who committed no crimes but happened to have been brought up in the wrong religion, or no religion.

Bishop John Shelby Spong apparently shared my impression. He wrote: "It was said 'God nailed his son to the cross for our salvation.' ... A human father who would nail his son to a cross for any purpose would be arrested for child abuse. ... I would choose to loathe rather than worship a deity who required the sacrifice of his son."[1]

Concerning the cross, Steven Pinker wrote: "It's more than a little macabre that a great moral movement would adopt as its symbol a graphic representation of a revolting means of torture and execution."[2] I had sometimes wondered if Jesus had been executed on a guillotine, would people then wear little gold ones on neck chains?

Later, when I developed the Bible-reading habit, I found even worse horrors. The Old Testament God never really meant it when he said, "Thou shalt not kill." On the contrary, again and again he ordered dreadful massacres of thousands of men, women, children, and animals, all to be slaughtered without mercy. He condoned rape, slavery, pillage, thievery, mutilation. He demanded the murder even of one's own family members if they were insufficiently respectful to him (Deut. 13:6-9). According to the Genesis story, he even destroyed the whole population of the earth in order to start over, when a few humans displeased him.

Far from inspiring love or adoration, this God struck me as the scariest character in all literature. An infinite egotist, demanding eternal praises, a jealous tyrant, a monument of cruelty, a constant threat. I wondered, how could anyone read the bible and not realize that its principal subject is a monster?

This question has puzzled me for most of my life. Might the answer be that God is so scary that people dared not criticize his behavior, out of the sheer terror euphemistically called "fear of God?" Thomas Paine remarked that the Bible is "a history of wickedness," and to his mind the Word of God looks more like the word of a demon.[3]

According to Robert Ingersoll, "Theology makes God a monster, a tyrant, a savage; makes man a servant, a serf, a slave; promises heaven to the obedient, the meek, the frightened, and threatens the self-reliant with the tortures of hell ... It seems almost impossible for religious people to really grasp the ideas of intellectual freedom."[4]

I don't understand why this fear is still allowed to infect children in a supposedly enlightened age. Nowadays, fundamentalist organizations like the Good News Club are still teaching young children to tell each other "You're going to hell" if they don't conform. Any psychologist knows that imaginary threats, however horrific, are not the key to good behavior. In my childhood experience they had only one result: I was presented with what seemed to be an imaginary fiend, and I blotted him out.

Let us hope for a future less tainted by God the Monster.

Notes

1. Spong, 95.
2. Pinker, 14.
3. Bufe, 208.
4. *Ibid.*, 174.

BEFORE PATRIARCHY

The world of prehistoric humanity has been largely misunderstood, due to the absurd mythologies presented in sacred literature, which were written by patriarchal revisionists with little knowledge of their own recent past, let alone the remote past. In pre-patriarchal times, many ancient beliefs connected superior intellect and magical skills with the female, based on the premise that only women possessed the ability to create life.

Noting that women ceased to discard their mysterious "moon blood" during pregnancy, ancient people logically reasoned that the baby was being made of that blood in the womb. Even in the Bible, menstrual blood is called the "flower" of the womb (Lev. 15:24), forerunner of the "fruit" of the womb (a child). Classical writers, like Pliny, continued to insist that every child was formed of a "curd" of menstrual blood. Aristotle called it a "coagulum," the primary substance of every "blood" relationship, which naturally proceeded through the female line. The ancients also believed that a postmenopausal woman became very wise as a result of keeping her "wise blood" within. In later centuries, this was used as a rationale for the magical sagacity of elder priestesses–who, of course, Christians condemned as witches for the very reason of their knowledge.

Through the Paleolithic and Neolithic periods, of course there was no such custom as monogamy, and the shifting sexual relationships of primitive groups recognized only maternal kinship bonds.

The nearest adult male relative of each child was the maternal uncle, the mother's brother, who possessed the same "blood" and was therefore intrinsic to the family. We still talk of blood ties, forgetting that there were no obvious "blood" relationships involving begetters. Like all social animals, early humans based their tribal connections on mothers and their offspring.

According to the principles of sympathetic magic, practiced by all ancient peoples, menstrual blood was the primary conception charm. It was used by women wishing to create a child; they would make a clay figure of a baby, and anoint it with menstrual blood to bring it to life. Such a charm underlay the very name of Adam, which translates as "bloody clay," though patriarchal scholars delicately prefer to style it "red earth."

Besides giving life, women established most of the civilized arts: the making of pottery and utensils, cultivating and storing food, creating the home place. It has been estimated that in hunter-gatherer societies, women provided up to 85 percent of the food. They also instituted fishing and planting, leading to the development of agriculture. Men went hunting, but apparently meat was not a daily staple of the primitive diet.

Branston says, "That societies in the past have arranged themselves on the principle that woman is the superior sex, we know well: in fact, it seems likely that until men found out their power of fertilization, woman was always regarded as superior ... succession in authority and property passing from mother to daughter. It is a natural state of affairs arising from a primitive ignorance of the part played in procreation by the male."[1]

The oldest traditions insist that language was a creation of the Goddess, given to ancient mothers. Pre-Hellenic Greece attributed the alphabet to the original three Muses, eponymous mothers of the elder tribes. The Latin alphabet was credited to the Goddess Carmenta, mother of *carmens*, which meant hymns, songs, and verbal charms. Hittites said writing was invented by the Gulses, or fate-mothers, who were similar to the old Germanic Fates known as *Die Schreiberinnen,* "the Writers." A later Roman title of the writing-goddess was *Fata Scribunda,* "the Fate who writes." According to the *Vaya Purana*, in ancient India "male ancestors" seemed to believe that language and arithmetic held the secret of women's fertility, and they told each other that they needed to learn the female skills of writing, measuring and figuring, so they might "happily create progeny."[2]

Ancient writings demonstrate that fatherhood was largely

unknown to early civilizations. Egyptians traced their descent through mothers, omitting the fathers' names and calling themselves, "X, born of the Lady Y." On Egyptian funerary steles, only the mother's name was given. In the earliest dynasties, the name of the Mother Goddess was a component of royal names, and the pharaoh's title was derived from *per aa*, the "Great Gate," a symbol of the cosmic womb.

Egyptian scriptures describe the Great Goddess as creator of the universe, "the Being eternal and infinite, the creative and ruling power of heaven, earth, and the underworld, and every creature ... Mother Goddess, lady of heaven, queen of the gods, who existed when nothing else had being, who created that which exists ... the greatest power on earth, who commandest all that is in the universe, and who preservest all the gods ... the God-Mother, giver of life, all that has been, that is, and that will be."[3] This last phrase is familiar as a biblical description of God in Revelation 1:8, but it was not original with the Bible. Long before the Bible was written, the phrase was carved in stone on the temple of the Great Mother at Sais.

All over the lands of antiquity, there were similar female divinities who overshadowed their sons or consorts, the gods. "The Great Mother Goddess was a towering figure who dominated the ancient world. In Egypt she was known as Isis and in Greece as Demeter. She was the mother or sister or spouse of Osiris-Dionysus or often, in that magical way that myth allows, all three. Gnostic mythology made her the third person of the Trinity, the Goddess Sophia (Wisdom), but also called her All-Mother, Mother of the Living, Shining Mother, the Power Above, the Holy Spirit ... In some Gnostic texts, the presumptuous Jehovah is scolded for his arrogance by his mother the Goddess Sophia."[4]

Like other ancient peoples, Egyptians made a great ceremony of a girl's first menstruation, indicative of her connection with the world-creating maternal power, just as in India she was said to bear the Kula flower, which united her with all the ancestresses. Like a number of other early peoples, Egyptians eventually instituted a similar bloodletting ceremony for adolescent boys, who were circumcised at the age of 13 so they too could shed some genital blood, in hopes of making them fertile. However, a boy on his way to this ceremony was dressed in girl's clothing, perhaps to find more favor with the Goddess.

The Hebrews copied the circumcision ceremony from the Egyptians but transferred it to infancy, while the actual pseudo-menarche ritual remained bloodless and evolved into the bar mitzvah. It is still said that in this ceremony the boy becomes a "son of the law," just as in ancient Egypt he became a "son of Maat," the traditional title of the lawgiving goddess. Many indigenous tribes of Africa, Polynesia, the Amazon area, and Australia practiced an even more painful version of circumcision, urethrotomy or penile subincision, and proudly referred to the wound as a "vagina." In some ancient myths, notably in South America, gods claimed to have given birth from genital wounds. In other cultures, as in northern Europe, gods were supposed to have given birth from wounds in their navels, thighs, or armpits. But somehow, sympathetic-magic fatherhood never really worked. Somehow, male blood just didn't have the same kind of zing.

Phoenicians, Sumerians and Babylonians wrote of a recent past when men didn't know their fathers, and took only the names of their mothers. In Babylon, the female took precedence in forms of address. The order of beings began with "Goddess and gods, women and men." The Lycians kept genealogical records of female names only, after the old custom, that was reversed by the biblical "begats."

Before the founding of Rome, Italy was governed by the Sabine matriarchate. Romulus, Ancus Marcus and Servius Tullius had no fathers, only mothers. When the myth of Romulus was written in the time of the empire, it said that his men were forced to marry the Sabine women because their *curiae* or "clans" were ancient "motherhoods," and only Sabine women possessed the *sanguis ac genus*, the "blood of the race." The Mother goddess of all clans was Juno Curiitis, the Queen of Heaven whom Rome adopted from the Sabines. Today's Roman popes pre-empted the same title and now call themselves a *curia*, but they trust the world to forget the primal meaning of that word, and they occupy an institution incongruously called Mother Church, ruled only by men.

Along with the spread of agricultural societies came the concept of male "seed" implanted in the female "Mother Earth" to produce fruit. The early idea of the savior god, whose body is grain and blood is wine, like Osiris, Adonis, and Dionysus, came from agricultural societies and created the idea of divine incest.

In other words, Mother Earth gives birth to this grain-god, who then re-enters her body as seed so she can give birth to him again. God the Father and God the Son are therefore made one in the body of Goddess the Mother. It makes sense as a metaphor for the cycles of nature, but it makes little sense in the Christian theology that inherited it, especially since the early church fathers disinherited the goddess altogether and made Mother Mary a mere human, even though the trinitarian God was still begetting himself through her, and the common people stubbornly persisted in worshiping her as divine.

In biblical terms, the magical blood of the womb was declared "unclean"–actually a rather inaccurate translation of the word meaning taboo, sacred, untouchable. Men were taught to fear this substance above all others. In medieval Europe it was forbidden for a woman even to enter a church if she was menstruating; clearly, not even God could protect his belongings from this terrible female "curse."

The Bible describes semen as "seed," while the body in which the seed was nurtured (the womb) was just soil, without any particular animating spirit. This was another way to denigrate women and belittle the very concept of motherhood, which the ancients had regarded as the original creative force. It was the first inkling of a system that could view fathers as more essential than mothers, a system that eventually erased the mother goddess from the collective psyche and set the stage for harsh father gods who threatened and punished their "children."

Men also came to believe that rather than female blood, male breath could be a magically animating principle. God had to say the magic Word, the *Logos*, to bring creation into existence. Hindus used to say that a father had to give his newborn child a soul by breathing into its face. Yet even the idea of the creative word was derived from ancient matriarchy: the great goddess of India voiced the word of creation, *Om*, which was her birth-giving *logos*. In Greece, the very alphabet ended with Om-mega, "Great Om," the promise of new birth as the cycle came around again.

Mythologies present various battles of the sexes, showing that patriarchy was not instituted without strife. The Norse Vanir or Elder Deities, led by Mother Freya, were attacked by new patriarchal deities from Aryan tribes, the Aesir, led by Father Odin. In the Aegean, followers of Father Zeus attacked the pre-Hellenic worshipers of Mother Rhea (or Hera), and revised the scriptures to force her into an unwanted marriage with the new *paterfamilias*. In Babyonian myth, the god Marduk fought against his own mother, Tiamat (whose name means "Goddess Mother"), and sliced her in half to form the heavens and the abyss: the "waters above the earth and the waters of the deeps," since Tiamat represented the mother-essence of the seas, water with the taste of blood.

This same Babylonian myth was copied into the Bible's creation story, where God "divided the waters which were under the firmament from the waters which were above the firmament" (Genesis 1:7). Of course Bible scholars are reluctant to admit that Yahweh was simply a cheap copy of Marduk, but even so they have diabolized the Mother Goddess Tiamat by describing her as a "dragon" slain by the young hero, and ignoring the assertion that she was the actual mother of the hero and all the other gods as well, and a creatress of the world.

The change from matriarchal to patriarchal orientations certainly didn't come overnight. Even in the Dark Ages, when Christian missionaries first traveled to the British Isles, they found tribes that did not recognize fatherhood and regarded the maternal uncle as the important relative. They had to refer to Jesus as "sister's son" to make him seem a worthwhile object of contemplation. (Even today, in French, a maternal uncle is called "own uncle," while a paternal uncle is just plain "uncle.")

Name-giving was a vital prerequisite for parental control of the young, and for patrilineal succession in property ownership, which is why we have so many English male "son" surnames: Peterson, Williamson, Richardson, Robertson, Stevenson, Clarkson–all designed to show who fathered the son, while the former matrilineal system of land ownership was being dismantled. Originally, the home place belonged to the mother (even among Hebrews, as shown by the Book of Ruth), and the father-god system enabled men to take it over. In ancient Egypt, a child's name was given by the mother along with her first breast milk, and even now some languages refer to a "milk name" as one given by a mother. In common with many ancient cultures, the early Irish believed that breast milk transmitted the soul to the baby along with its name. Up to the twelfth century, the Irish still baptized with milk, until in 1172 the Synod of Cashel banned the practice and insisted that baptism can be performed only by a priest.[5] Transition from male to female nomenclature is a sure sign of patriarchal beginnings.

Myths speak often of violent attacks of male deities. This legend of leadership being wrested from the women, by force or coercion, is too widely spread throughout the world to be buried by scholars who should know better. According to Engels, "The overthrow of mother-right was the world-historic downfall of the female sex."

Yet in ways not immediately apparent, it may have been the downfall of the male sex also. It brought essential changes in social attitudes which have been extremely destructive. The violence, intolerance, and ruthless power-seeking characteristic of patriarchal societies seem to have been largely absent from the earlier matricentric ones, where people seem to have lived more comfortably together.

When all people were thought related by blood to the same mother, they were universal siblings and restrained from shedding that blood in another. Some past societies dreaded even a temporary loss of the divine mother image. Of the seasons when the goddess departed from the world, Apuleius wrote: "There has been no pleasure, no joy anywhere ... Wedlock and true friendship and parents' love for their children have vanished from the earth; there is one vast disorder and foul disregard for the bonds of love."[6]

When the goddess image was permanently displaced from human awareness, a sense of alienation became a cultural norm. Robert Briffault gives us food for thought when he says, "The maternal totemic clan was by far the most successful form that human association has assumed—it may indeed be said that it has been the only successful one."[7]

No doubt a return to respect for the mother goddess image as a metaphor for the earth on which we all depend, every one of us, always, from birth to death, would not be at all out of place in our upstart patriarchal world.

Notes

1. Branston, 130.
2. O'Flaherty, 48.
3. Budge 1, 213.
4. Freke & Gandy, TJM, 93-94.
5. Condren, 171.
6. Neumann, A & P, 31.
7. Briffault 2, 493.

THE THREE AGES OF WOMAN

Humanoids have existed on this planet for almost three million years, but only in the last five thousand of those years have they become aware of fatherhood, and so envisioned a creator god as a begetter. In earlier times, among humans as among all other mammals, the only recognized parent was a mother. Therefore, the only all-creating deity known to our early ancestors was a mother goddess.

Five thousand years is an almost infinitesimal fraction, one six-hundredth of our three million years of existence as a mammalian species. That leaves 599/600 when females were viewed as the universal source, and male father gods were unknown. For Stone Age children, the important male relative was the mother's brother, with whom they recognized kinship through the essential maternal blood bond.

Societies based on this notion of gender function were quite different from the patriarchal societies known today. They were less competitive and less violent, more relaxed and cooperative. When men worshiped a supreme Goddess as a nurturant, birth-giving Mother, they seem to have been more at ease with each other and with their natural environment. Artifacts from early matriarchal civilizations, in such places as Catal Huyuk, Sumer, Minoan Crete, and the Indus Valley show almost no weapons or scenes of violence. Early myths reveal that it was usually taken for granted that all forms of love, as well as interpersonal and group relationships, were founded on the bond between mother and child.

Hindus called this bond *karuna*, mother love. They claimed that every worthwhile and pleasant thing, from sexuality to spiritual awareness and intellect depended on it. Sexuality was perceived as a blessing rather than a sin: a means whereby men could make contact with the divine force in women, and sexual partners could achieve a foretaste of heavenly bliss.

The original goddess was immanent rather than transcendent. She had three distinct cyclic phases, the trinity of Virgin, Mother, and Crone, based on the three ages of woman that are set off by menarche, childbirth, and menopause. All over the ancient world, these three Goddess *personae* were represented by the colors white, red, and black.[1]

In ancient India these colors represented the *gunas*, intricately interwoven strands of fate, sometimes viewed as the white and black of days and nights bound together by the ongoing blood-red thread of life. Classical Greek and Roman writers also called white, red, and black the colors of the threads of life, or of destiny. Theocritus, Ovid, Tibullus and Horace all said the sacred colors of the life-threads were white, red, and black.

The three female thread-spinning and weaving Fates of Greek, Roman, Persian, Teutonic, and Scandinavian mythology were other versions of the same trinitarian goddess said to rule the fates of all people. Shakespeare's three witches were descendants of the Saxon fate-goddess named Wyrd, or Destiny, hence they were the Weird Sisters. Similar folklore figures were the fairy godmothers who decided the fate of each individual at birth. Even Snow White, with her skin white as snow, lips red as blood, and hair black as ebony recalled the colors of the original holy trinity.

Because they were known to be of pagan origin, and to have something to do with goddess tradition, the three colors were often diabolized in Christian lore, as when Dante made them the colors of Lucifer's three heads. Nevertheless, Christian authorities copied the colors of the Virgin, Mother, and Crone in the white, red, and black veils laid over church altars for Christmas matins. The same three colors pop up again and again in fairy tales and folklore.

The first of the old goddess's three personae, the Virgin, was nothing like our present definition of the term. She was not perceived as a physical virgin. The old Latin word *virgines*, like the Greek *parthenos*, meant only women who were unmarried and independent of male control. Like the virgin goddess Athene, who had a number of lovers, she was her own person. A Greek descendant of the old Libyan triple goddess, Athene as heavenly virgin had her own temple, the Parthenon, which means Virgin-House. Modern visitors to that once-magnificent shrine usually are not told that it was a goddess temple.

Priestesses who played the role of sacred harlots in the temples were given the title of virgins. Their children, often begotten by the priests, were known as virgin-born offspring of the deity. For centuries, throughout the ancient world there were large numbers of traditional holy virgins who were both brides and mothers of gods.

The word used for "virgin" Mary in the bible is a bad translation of the original *almah*, which meant only a young woman, possibly a temple attendant or *kadesha*. The same word in Persian referred to the unmarried but abundantly sexual moon goddess. Rome's famous vestal virgins were temple priestesses, who tended the all-important perpetual flame that represented Rome's continued existence. In times of the later (patriarchal) empire they were expected to preserve their chastity for life, but that seems not to have been the case in earlier times, when the high priest (*pontifex maximus*) consummated their marriage to the phallic deity of the Palladium.[2]

A seldom noticed aspect of the holy virgin image is that she is never depicted as a child. To pagan and Christian alike, the virgin was full grown and able to take responsibility for the male god who appeared as a baby more often than not. The ubiquitous virgin-mother-and-child dyad from classical mythology up to the present shows the primary human bond of *karuna*, in which the male is the helpless, dependent one. The original virgin mother, at the root of mythologies the world over, is virgin because she was the sole creator, without a consort. She made the universe and all its gods, who were her sons. Myths tell how, after they grew, she took one or many of them as lovers.

This is the first, oldest version of divine incest in which the goddess unites God the Father and God the Son through her own person, as both mother and mate. The Christian version of divine incest is seldom recognized as such, but it is plainly spelled out in the dogma that says God and his Son are united through the intermediary of the Mother/Bride, in the same manner as Horus was united with his father Osiris by his mother-bride Isis, and Adonis with his father Eros by his mother-bride Aphrodite/Myrrha.

During the Gnostic period in Christian Rome, church authorities forbade worship of the mortal Mary, on the ground that no mortal woman should ever be worshiped. But they adopted the birthgiving goddess figure by way of her symbol, the white dove, which represented sexual passion and was the ancient totem of Venus Columba, Aphrodite Marina, and other images of the impassioned virgin.[3]

The pagan idea of a trinitarian father-mother-son deity was not accepted by early church fathers until they were able to turn the third person into a male, the Holy Ghost or Holy Spirit, which was almost devoid of personality but managed to destroy the formerly logical interrelationships of the holy family. They retained the dove, which no longer represented the passion of Aphrodite but became a white symbol of purity (quite in opposition to the actual nature of doves).

Originally, the idea of a dying-and-resurrecting father/son god grew from agricultural societies in a fairly rational symbolization of nature. Mother Earth gave birth to the crops, which were consumed by the worshipers, and their seeds were replanted in the same tomb-womb that gave them birth, to be resurrected as the next year's crop. Emblems of the god thus born, slain, and reborn were typically bread and wine for his "flesh" and "blood", and his semen was regarded as "seed" (as in the biblical term). Thus in dying, the savior god impregnated his own Mother Earth and gave a new life to himself. Divine incest was a fairly accurate representation of agriculture, though it became nonsensical when applied to the human family.

To comprehend old pagan ideas of the virgin we must return to that first 599/600 of humanity's existence and ask, if they didn't know about physical fatherhood, how did they think babies were made?

The answer is to be found in hundreds of myths, customs, and folkloric superstitions. The real life force was supposed to reside in menstrual blood, given to all women by the moon mother because it followed the moon's phases. Observing that a woman kept this blood within her body during gestation of a child, our ancestors naturally figured that the child was being made of this blood. Hence, such biblical expressions as "the blood is the life" or "the life of all flesh is in the blood thereof." The very idea of blood kinship used to refer only to the female line. Aristotle stated that every human life is made of a "coagulum" of menstrual blood, and Pliny the Elder also said a baby's body is formed from a "curd" of menstrual blood.[4]

Old creation myths show that the original virgin creatress prepared to form the universe from her own ocean of blood, or red sea, or in the Homeric phrase, "the wine-dark sea." Babylonians and Sumerians said that the Goddess menstruated for the trinitarian period of three years and three months to produce enough holy blood to bring all life forms into existence. Some said that seawater, which tastes like blood, was the effluent of the Goddess's womb; thus myths often related female divinity to the ocean (which is, indeed, the original source of all life).

Interestingly, the "fire and water" male-female element combination grew from a notion that seawater could become blood when fertilized and reddened by "fire from heaven": *i.e.*, lightning, the phallic symbol of Lucifer the "Light-Bringer," Zeus, Agni, Jehovah and other "fiery" gods. The mythic concept was retained in Christianity even after its pagan origins were forgotten. The Virgin Mary was symbolized by the font, consecrated by a burning paschal candle being quenched in its waters, with the words "May a heavenly offspring, conceived in holiness and reborn into a new creation, come forth from the stainless womb of this divine font." The Virgin Mary was then said to have been "fecundated by the sacred fire," just like her forerunner Aphrodite Marina (the white dove) and other primal sea goddesses of antiquity.[5]

In India, when a young girl received the first touch of her divine life-giving power at her menarche, she was said to have borne the *kula* flower, connecting her to the family bonds of blood. There were elaborate rituals to celebrate the occasion. Menstrual blood as the red "flower" of the womb is the forerunner of the "fruit" (a child); the same symbolism occurs in the Old Testament. (Lev. 15:24) The white lily and the red rose were often associated with the virgin Goddess, the latter standing for Hindu *sattva*, the sacred blood with the power to produce life.

Throughout prehistory and history, men regarded this sacred blood with awe, fear, and envy, and often tried to imitate it by sympathetic magic. The Egyptian god Ra enabled himself to give birth by cutting his penis to produce blood. So did the Aztec god Quetzalcoatl. Men evolved penis-cutting rituals for boys, to be done while the girls were having their menarche ceremonies. Among Australian aborigines, the painful operation of subincision was inflicted on thirteen-year-old boys while the girls were being honored. A boy's wound was therefore called a "vagina" and his bloodletting was "man's menstruation."[6]

In ancient Egypt, thirteen-year-old boys were circumcised for their ritual bloodletting, but while going to the ceremony they were dressed as girls.[7] According to Herodotus, the Jews copied circumcision from the Egyptians but changed its time to infancy, as dictated by Moses, whose wife did not like it and called him a "bloody husband" (Ex. 4:25). They retained the pubescent part of the ceremony as the bar mitzvah, an "initiation into manhood" just as the girls were being initiated by Mother Nature into womanhood. The Egyptians regarded circumcision as a representation of the boy as a "son of Ma'at," that is, the Goddess in her lawgiving aspect; so the bar mitzvah makes a boy "son of the law." While thus honoring the official maturation of the boy, patriarchal custom indicated that a mother must give her daughter a slap instead of a party on the occasion of her menarche, to remind her that femaleness is sinful.

Some ancient societies sacrificed a man at important intervals, especially in the season of spring planting: placing the "seed" into its earth-tomb-womb for resurrection, and at the same time induced genital bleeding by castration, as in the myths of Attis and Adonis.

Apparently it was thought for a long time that males, in order to be really fertile, had to look like females in one way or another.

In Greece, the very gods themselves were kept alive by infusions of "supernatural red wine" given them by Hebe, the virgin form of Great Mother Hera.[8] In India also, the gods "rose blessed to the heavens" after drinking blood from the virgin Goddess. Many myths speak of the first father gods stealing magic blood from the Goddess. Blood sacrifices to the gods, to keep them alive, are ubiquitous in mythology. The biblical Yahweh insisted on receiving the blood of every sacrifice, which was poured out solely for him on the altar and forbidden to humans; this was the origin of kosher killing of meat animals.

Along with male efforts to imitate, colonize, or take over female blood magic when many indications of male dread of the real thing. The Bible strictly forbids men all contact with menstrual blood, calling it "unclean," a rather inaccurate translation of the original words for taboo, untouchable, or sacred.[9] Jewish and Christian strictures against the "pollution" of menstrual blood are so numerous and so apparently frightening even to God, that to list them would take volumes.

Throughout the Middle Ages, a menstruating woman was forbidden to set foot in a church, because her very presence would make God uncomfortable. To disobey this rule was declared a mortal sin.[10] As late as 1684, church records still speak of menstruating women standing outside the church door, unable to enter. Albert the Great, Thomas Aquinas, Duns Scotus and other theological authorities asserted that any child conceived during a menstrual period would be deformed, leprous, crippled, or demonic. In the late seventeenth century, sexual intercourse with a menstruating women was still considered a mortal sin, though it was later demoted to a venial sin. In the twelfth century, Chancellor Odo at the University of Paris ruled that if a wife tries to tempt her husband into lovemaking at such times, he should "keep her impudence down with fasts and beatings."[11]

"The stroke of genius that allowed ecclesiastical power to succeed was achieved when the pervasive human guilt over inadequacy and failure was connected to the universal human reality of desire, especially sexual desire ... Holiness was defined as sexlessness. ... women were made to feel guilty because they were women, guilty if they menstruated, guilty if they loved a man, guilty if they got married, guilty if they had children ... Men were made to feel guilty for having any sexual desires, guilty for having power, guilty for loving a woman."[12]

For all the fear and horror generated by the female mysteries of menstruation and birth, some bizarre myths show that men tried to imagine gods giving birth, to confirm their power over life. The Greeks' sky god Zeus was alleged to have given birth to Athene from his head, and Dionysus from his thigh; but in both cases he first swallowed the true mother during her pregnancy. The Norse god Loki gave birth from his heart (formerly considered the actual source of woman's "magic blood"). The Scandinavian earth-giant Ymir gave birth from his armpit. Several Egyptian gods gave birth from their mouths. The Hindu god Shiva gave birth from his penis.

Primitive societies sometimes instituted the custom of couvade, whereby a husband would lie down and moan and groan and puff while his wife was in labor, and pretend to deliver the child. Afterward, he would remain convalescent, receiving gifts and congratulations from his friends while the real mother got up and went back to work.

The biblical story of Adam's birth-giving from his rib was derived from the Sumero-Babylonian myth of the goddess Nin-Ti, "Lady of the Rib," who caused babies' bones to be formed *in utero* by one of the mother's ribs.[13] But one of the same goddess's titles, "Mother of All Living," was given to Eve, who was said by several Gnostic sources to be the mother of Adam, and even of Jehovah himself.[14] Adam's name is usually misleadingly translated "red earth," but its precise meaning is "bloody clay," recalling the popular fertility charm of primitive women, making a clay figure of a baby and anointing it with menstrual blood to create a real baby by sympathetic magic. No male was involved. Not having the requisite blood, the Biblical God had to use breath: to animate

Adam's clay by his magic word, the *logos*. But in the Koran, sura 23:12-14, God is said to have made man from "an extract of clay, then we made him a clot (of) of congealed blood," which then grew into bone and flesh.[15] Isn't it strange that God would have recourse to such ancient female magic?

Spretnak says: "Patriarchy is based on the 'phallacy' that the male is creator. Man's original awe and envy of woman becomes, under patriarchy, resentment and hostility ... Patriarchy is indeed a male neurosis. Every social institution under male dominance is an expression of man's womb envy, designed to take woman's power away from her and place it in the hands of men. In squelching female energy, patriarchy creates a culture that is destructive and death-oriented ... While woman sheds the Blood of Life each moon at menstruation, man can only shed the blood of death through warfare and killing."[16]

Patriarchal revisionists wanted to make begetting more important than birthgiving, hence the biblical "begats" comprised of long lists of fictional male ancestors, without any listing of mothers. Ironically, however, the lists include many female names that were simply copied from older scriptures by ignorant scribes. Male anxiety to usurp maternal functions is demonstrated by the biblical vision of a "nursing father" carrying the "sucking child" in his bosom (Num. 11:12).

Like menstruation, birthgiving was dreaded by Christian authorities, who ruled that a new mother may not enter a church for forty days after giving birth to a boy, or eighty days if the child is a girl, following the law laid down in Leviticus 12. During this period, both mother and child were considered "impure" and dangerous for priests to touch. At the expiration of this period the child could be baptized, but if it died beforehand, it was called demonic and automatically consigned to eternal suffering in hell.

God's cruelty in this respect was later mitigated by the invention of limbo, a holding tank for unbaptized infants, pending the parents' purchase of suitable incantations from the priest. Medieval women, however, sometimes spurned the condemnation of the upstart Christian God and remembered their pagan roots, saying that their unbaptized infants actually went to the care of the underground mother, Frau Holda, or the goddess Hel, the underground Crone aspect of the great mother.[17]

Hel was the third person of the trinity, the Scandinavian dark goddess, supreme ruler of the underworld (*i.e.*, hell), which was not envisioned as a place of punishment but simply the land of the dead. She led the deified pagan ancestors known as *helleder*, or hellmen. Variations of her name were Helle, Holle, Hild, Frau Holde, Helga; her sacred plant, the holly, bore blood-red berries and was revered for remaining green with life at the midwinter solstice (Yule). A church council ruled that no one should bring holly into the house at Christmas, because it was a custom of "heathen people."[18] Her genital-symbolic pit, "Holle's Well," was once said to be the source of all children on earth.

As the third of the trinity of Fates, Hel also had the Anglo-Saxon name of Wyrd, or Destiny, which was applied to the threefold sisterhood of witches around their cauldron. A primary symbol of death and rebirth, the black cauldron was associated with the underground goddess as the tomb-womb, representing a basic theological difference between paganism and Christianity.

While Christian lore insisted that life must end in a single, unalterable choice between heaven and hell, parts of the pagan world believed in continual recycling of living forms in the eternally churning cauldron of nature. Hel's children were dissolved, recombined, and born again in other life forms. It was a primitive version of biochemical knowledge, derived from observation of nature rather than from ecclesiastical dicta.

Ancestor worship also involved reverence for the environment, of which the ancestors became a part. Like Native American traditions, the religion of Hel sacralized earth, air, animals, and the underworld where all forms were recycled into their various appearances on earth.

Hel was also the Crone, symbolizing the postmenopausal elder woman, who was often a seeress or high priestess. The theory behind the eminence of elder women in pagan societies was the same as that of menstrual blood: when women ceased to menstruate, they retained within their bodies that magical blood that knew how to create life, and so became very wise.

Even early Hebrew tribes had a period when they were governed by elder wise-women, as shown by biblical stories like that of Deborah, who "judged" all of Israel, and Sarah, whose name is a queenly title,[19] and Naomi, who determined the names of tribal children.

In Egypt, the title of an elder matriarchal wise-woman was *hek*, and her magical commanding "words of power" were known as *hekau*, the forerunner of the witch's enchantments. The ancient Egyptian goddess of the dead migrated to Greece as Hecate, queen of the underworld, one of whose titles was "Mistress of Spells." Revisionist myths of the patriarchal period claimed that the gods plunged Hecate into the river Styx to cleanse her of the dreaded contagion of the birth chamber (she was also the Divine Midwife) and she remained in the underworld to rule the souls of the dead, an alternate version of Persephone.

Hecate became one of the most feared figures of medieval Christian mythology, which designated her Queen of Witches. Most churchmen earnestly believed in her reality. Innumerable elder women were tortured and burned for the crime of communicating with Hecate, especially midwives. Catholic handbooks said "no one does more harm to the Catholic faith than midwives," and taught that the midwives baptized newborn children into the service of the devil.[20] It is even possible that some midwives—members of the only profession open in medieval times only to elder women, never to men—did remember their pagan traditions and prayed to Hecate the Queen of Midwives, instead of to the Christian God who imposed childbirth as a curse on women (Gen. 3:16).

In Europe, elder women had always served as midwives and healers in general. Christian doctors refused to have anything to do with childbirth, and as a rule treated only members of the upper classes rather than the peasants, who were left to consult the village wise-women. Both Francis Bacon and Thomas Hobbes wrote that the wise-women were much better doctors than the "learned physicians." Hobbes said he would rather have the advice of, and take physic from, "an experienced old woman" rather than consult a university-trained doctor. Such doctors "played a prominent role in the witchcraft persecutions...in order to eliminate competition from lay healers and midwives."[21]

Christianity had brought to Europe an entirely new attitude toward death. There were no more natural cycles. Each human life remained distinct from all other life forms. There was to be no mingling of human, plant, and animal substance in Hecate's cauldron, despite the fact that such diverse substances do become part of one another in the mere processes of living and dying. Conflict between these views of life and death gave rise to a thousand years of bitter ideological warfare, even though Christians themselves continued to harbor superstitious beliefs in earthly reincarnations, such as werewolves, vampires, ghosts, familiar spirits, and other entities associated with the Queen of Witches.

She was worshiped especially at Halloween, the Eve of All Hallows, known in the old lunar calendar as Samhain, the Feast of the Dead. Priestesses of the underworld goddess used to call up the spirits of dead ancestors, to give them thanks and pay them homage in the season of harvest. The church renamed the holy day after their own calendar of All Saints, but the pagan Eve kept the old connotations: hence the Hallows-Eve witches and their attendant ghosts, those pagan ancestors whom the church now declared to be demons. The Halloween jack-o-lantern began as the real skull of an honored ancestor on the table of the harvest dinner (the "death's head at the feast"), which often had a candle placed within to represent the "light" of a conscious spirit.

Just as the knowledge of inevitable death continued to haunt even those who pretended to believe in eternal joy in heaven–but more often deeply dreaded eternal suffering in hell–so also the idea of the black Crone continued to scare even those who claimed their faith in God would save them. Nothing in patriarchal mythology shows quite so passionate a denial of nature as the effort to suppress the Crone figure and all she stood for. That's why elder women, midwives, widows, and village wise-women were legally murdered by the thousands; and that's why, though impossibly combined as they are, we still have remnants of the Virgin and Mother figures, and the Crone has been suppressed almost beyond recovery.

Yet in eastern cultures there is evidence that the black Crone was the true culmination of the Goddess's trinity. In India, where she was known as the black Goddess Kali Ma, the Destroyer, the god himself was shown under her feet as she devoured him. Her icons wield the symbols of the four elements; her necklace of skulls bears the original letters of the Sanskrit alphabet, prototype of all the *Logos* magic of creation, whereby she brought the universe into being.

The scriptures of Kali Ma say: "His Goddess, his loving Mother in time, who gives him birth and loves him in the flesh, also destroys him in the flesh. His image of her is incomplete if he does not know her as his tearer and devourer."[22]

The trinitarian nature of Kali Ma is clearly revealed in many scriptural descriptions. It was said that "The Divine Mother first appears as her worshiper's earthly mother, then as his wife; thirdly as Kalika, she reveals herself in old age, disease and death."[23] Her white Virgin and red Mother aspects were swallowed up in the Crone's black, for, her worshipers said, all colors are consumed by the ultimate darkness. Yet she was not wholly fearsome, like Europe's Queen of Witches. One of the poems honoring her was attributed to the god Vishnu:

> Material cause of all change, manifestation, and destruction, the whole Universe rests upon Her, rises out of Her and melts away into Her. From Her are crystallized the original elements and qualities which construct the apparent worlds. She is both mother and grave...The gods themselves are merely constructs out of Her maternal substance, which is both consciousness and potential joy.[24]

Parvati-Durga-Kali, Hebe-Hera-Hecate, Juventas-Juno-Minerva, Kore-Demeter-Persephone, the Graces, the Muses, the Fates—the earliest versions of the Holy Trinity seem to have been female, the original symbol of the Creator-Preserver-Destroyer Mother Earth, who gives produces, nourishes, and finally devours all life. Male trinities never made the same kind of symbolic sense.

In modern Western tradition the signs of female aging are often seen as repugnant; more so than the signs of male aging. Women have been taught to deny or disguise the latter third of their life cycle. Despite these destructive trends, instituted by patriarchy, some women have learned a real sense of power that accompanies cessation of their menses, signaling entry into a newly autonomous phase of life. Some can restore to its ancient honor the title of Crone, to apply it to themselves and to glory in it. Even in a society that still finds the term "old crone" pejorative, there are elder women learning to celebrate themselves and menopause rituals, finding a new awareness of the feminine spirit.

Notes

1. Wedeck, 66.
2. Dumezil, 583.
3. Turville-Petre, 109.
4. Briffault 2, 444.
5. Legman, 55.
6. Gifford, 93.
7. Briffault 3,332.
8. Graves 1, 118.
9. Abelard, 19.
10. Morris, 110.
11. Ranke-Heinemann, 23-25, 195.
12. Spong, 90-91.
13. Hooke, 115.
14. Pagels, 57-58.
15. Warraq, 135.
16. Spretnak, 401-402.
17. Miles, 242.
18. Briffault 3, 110.
19. Hazlitt, 118, 127.
20. Kramer & Sprenger, 66, 141.
21. Noble, 203, 218.

22. Rawson, A.T., 184.
23. *Ibid.*, 183.
24. Rawson, E.A., 159.

THE STAR IN THE EAST

Thousands of years ago in the land of Egypt, people waited anxiously every year for the natural event on which all their lives depended: the annual flooding of the Nile, which brought blessed water to irrigate their fields.

The water came more than four thousand miles from melting snows in the Ruwenzori, which means "Mountains of the Moon." Egyptians knew little about those distant places beyond their southern horizon, where there were trackless swamps and dark jungles. But they did say all waters came from the moon, which they envisioned as the lifegiving breast of Mother Isis, who gave birth to the savior. Another title of the Moon Mother was Nut, the goddess of the sky; her breasts produced the Milky Way composed of all the stars.

The savior was the god Osiris, who embodied the grain that grew in their irrigated fields. Every year he died in the reaping, and was born again as the new wheat sprouted. His flesh was the bread, his blood was the wine. People thought they could become godlike by eating him sacramentally; then they could go after death to the paradise of Osiris, where they could live in eternal happiness.

Osiris was also identified with his father Ra, the sun god, and so was born at the winter solstice. The father/son amalgamation of Ra/Osiris formed a holy trinity with Isis, the holy mother. In the Gnostic period, even Christians viewed the third person of the trinity as female, depicting her as the dove, an ancient Goddess totem. Though she was later masculinized as the Holy Spirit, and the all-male trinity accepted by the early church, they eventually adopted the official solstitial birthday of the sun as their own version of the savior's birth. (No writings of any kind had ever mentioned any official birthday for Jesus.)

Egyptian legends told of a time when the Nile flood had failed for seven years in a row. The land dried up. There was no food; many people starved to death. (The seven-year famine also made its way into the Old Testament.) Such stories reminded everyone of the vital importance of grain storage techniques, and also of the vital necessity of the Nile flood.

Egyptian priests and priestesses anxiously studied the night sky, to learn from this celestial calendar just when the rising of the waters could be expected. Over the centuries they allegorized their observations. They noted that the star Sirius, the brightest star in the sky, rose in the east about the time that the flood was due, so they identified this star with the coming of Osiris. They called this star Sothis, and associated it with Anubis the Great Dog, jackal god of the dead, who held the soul of Osiris and prepared him for his annual rebirth. We still call Sirius the Dog Star, and its constellation Canis Major, the Great Dog.

Egyptians also identified the three wise men who pointed the way to the savior's birth: the three stars in the belt of Orion: Mintaka, Anilam, and Alnitak, which rise ahead of Sirius and lie in a line pointing directly toward it. They said the three wise men had seen the star of Osiris in the east and announced his coming. When the savior was born, the Egyptians celebrated the Festival of the Inundation, rejoicing at the savior's birth and honoring the holy mother and child with a traditional chant: "The virgin has brought forth! The savior is born!"

In summoning the spirit of the new grain from the earth, God said, "Out of the land of Egypt I have called my son"–a phrase considered prophetic by gospel writers who invented a flight into Egypt for their holy family, just so Jesus could be said to have come from there.

The reason given in the gospels for their flight, King Herod's attack on newborn children, was quite impossible because Herod died in 4 BCE.

Eventually the three wise men received the Persian title of magi, (*i.e.*, sacred magicians) from the religion of the Zoroastrian savior Mithra, to whom the priests presented symbolic birthday gifts of gold, frankincense and myrrh. Christians pretended that the magi traveled from their eastern land to present these tokens to the new savior.

Since Bethlehem lies far to the west of Persia, isn't it odd that the three wise men got there by following a star in the east?

WHAT IS A SOUL?

The term "soul" has many meanings. It may refer to the inner self, or what Hindus call the *atman*, the "god within," or spirit, or life force in general. It may describe our emotional/esthetic sense, our response to nature, to beauty, to music, to love, or to any experience that we find thrilling or uplifting. Some regard it as a sense of connection between our individual consciousness and the universe of which we are a part. Consciousness is usually regarded as a characteristic essential to nearly all definitions of "soul."

Many primitive people believed that during sleep, trance, or coma the soul leaves the body and goes wandering, to experience what are perceived as dreams. Australian aborigines used to describe their dreams as actual happenings, as real as any waking events. Throughout history, most of the world believed that the soul must leave the body not only in sleep but also at the time of death, and go elsewhere–either into another body, or into an after-life in a different state. In that different state, however, the soul was supposed to retain various bodily functions such as seeing, hearing, speaking, or even a complete nervous system, necessary to feel the agonies of hell or the bliss of heaven. Never mentioned were the functions of digestion or elimination; apparently the soul can have eyes and ears but no intestines.

Here is where we become irrational. What creature could see without eyes, hear without ears, speak without vocal cords, or feel without nerves? Reason has to be abandoned in the effort to envision this, a circumstance never seen or known, but only hoped for. As humans, we like to think that whatever impossibility we can imagine must be somehow true in reality. Hence our ubiquitous beliefs in impossibilities like fairies, vampires, werewolves, trolls, elves, gnomes, angels, demons, dragons, dryads and gods.

The real difficulty in this concept of the soul is that it arises from language itself. Human beings invent words for the nonexistent, then use the words themselves as proof of existence. The word "soul" is one of thousands of words that we use in this way. But if we use the word "soul" to refer to our emotional response to beauty, inspiration, or inner feelings, then "soul" is *not an entity, but a function*. It is not a thing but a process—a function of the assembled neurons in the brain—the sum total of our memories, sensations, experiences, desires, fears, and other emotional responses. Just as without a stomach we don't digest, without a physical brain we don't have consciousness. Consciousness is what the brain does, just as digestion is what the stomach does, sight is what the eyes do, hearing is what the ears do, and so on. We are conscious only because there are trillions of electrochemical impulses constantly being exchanged between living neurons in our brains. Our awareness is like music played on an instrument; without the instrument, there is no music.

Those who wish to retain the concept of a soul as a different entity, somehow separable from the brain, often postulate some completely unknown form of electromagnetic energy that can reproduce all the brain functions without any physical ground. But of course there is no evidence whatever for any such energy. It is as unrealistic as the unicorn, as ephemeral as the phoenix, as empty as the void. It describes nothing. Souls of the dead–ghosts–abound in legend and story, but have never been conclusively authenticated and never will be, because they exist only in human imaginings.

The concept of an immortal soul is primarily our own self-aware ego convincing itself that it can never become nonexistent. The idea is unthinkable, so we try not to think it. Just as the inner parent image is transformed into a mother goddess or father god, so the inner self-image becomes the *atman*: the self that we think too uniquely wonderful ever to dissolve like every other life form. Thus, in our egotism, we set ourselves above all the laws of the known universe.

Since every life form strives for its own continued existence, it might be said that life is basically about staying alive. But only human beings manage to convince themselves that they might be able to do it forever, despite the contrary evidence that nature shows them every day. No living thing lives forever. Even if it is not killed by disease, or by becoming food for another life, every living thing eventually declines into death. The idea that humans might be exempt from this law of nature is fatuous enough to cast considerable doubt on our vaunted learning abilities. Our religious authorities keep insisting (because their livelihood depends on it) that we must have "faith" in the kind of immortal soul that they postulate. But in truth, no amount of faith can make the physically impossible become physically possible.

To be truly proud of our human intelligence, we ought to use it to better purpose than to postulate ego-soothers like the immortal soul, and spend it on devising ways to improve our culture, develop our mindfulness, care for our environment, and end our wars. For highly evolved creatures, humans have been much too foolish for much too long. If the undeniable fact that we have but one life were to become the general understanding of all humanity, surely we would not want to sacrifice it in useless battles, or waste it on needless hostilities.

Very often we hear people sidestepping the problem of the soul by confessing that "I'm not religious, but I'm very spiritual." This seems to refer to the emotional/esthetic responses in general, but what do we really mean by spirituality? It's a portmanteau word with different meanings as defined by different people. Webster's preferred definitions tie it to organized religion, even in the eminently material sense of "ecclesiastical property or revenue," and "fees, dues or tithes receivable by an ecclesiastic." Money, apparently, is spiritual rather than material as long as a church has it.

But Webster's sixth definition seems to contradict the first: "spiritual as distinguished from a worldly or material character." However, defining "spirituality" as "spiritual" doesn't get us very far.

Few churches, with the possible exception of Unitarians, encourage congregations to define or discuss their spirituality any more than they encourage discussion of theology. Freud defined spirituality as "the oceanic feeling," meaning that swelling, uplifted inner sense that may be experienced while listening to music, watching a sunset, meditating, or other oneness-with-the-universe moments. The feeling can be produced artificially by drugs or drunkenness, which is why people throughout the ages have been enthusiastic about both. (Indeed, the word "enthusiasm" by derivation means the same as *atman*, "the god within.")

Another eternally popular kind of high is sexual bliss, which was also once considered an ultimate expression of spirituality. Strongly ascetic tendencies of Judeo-Christian culture have taught the civilized world to think of spirituality and sexuality as opposites: the holy versus the carnal. But among the ancient Greeks and Romans, the rites of Aphrodite or of Venus were regarded as the foretaste of paradise, thoughtfully provided by the Goddess. Such rites were often practiced on Friday, the day named in English from the Goddess's northern counterpart, Freya. People ate fish on that day because fish were considered aphrodisiac food, symbolic of female genitalia (the so-called fish sign or *vesica piscis*, the pointed-oval now widely used as a symbol of Jesus).[1] The Catholic church adopted the fish-eating custom because people were used to it, but gave it a radically different interpretation.

The so-called love feast–*agape* in Greek–was based on sacred sex, the same ritual known as *maithuna* in Tantric Buddhism. Early Gnostic Christians continued to practice a sexual *agape* up to the sixth century, when it was denounced as heretical and a stimulus for massacre of Gnostics. Of course, Christian authorities never had any equally potent description of the bliss of paradise, though they were exhaustively specific about the agonies of hell.

Aside from organized religion, what are we to make of those whose inner spiritual sense leads them to allegedly direct communication with UFO aliens, or Ascended Masters, or angels, or demons, or Atlantean priests, or a personal God? What about the lunatic whose god tells him to murder his neighbor? Or for that matter, the perfectly sane soldier whose god tells him to kill thousands of innocents? What about the fanatic who knows beyond any shadow of a doubt that Doomsday will arrive a year from next Thursday and Jesus is coming in person to fetch him?

If spirituality is whatever enhances our lives with imagination and feeling, are not the experiences of the kooks and crazies equally valid? How can we distinguish between "genuine" spirituality and nuttiness?

Thus spirituality and superstition may be entwined, while both may overlap with faith. Faith means believing without hard evidence, yet rationality must demand hard evidence, or at least compelling probability, as a prerequisite to faith. Therefore most superstitions do their adherents the notable disservice of stifling thought in favor of that ignorance which is, if not bliss, at least blessed.

We might consider soulless those so-called spiritual leaders who deliberately prey on the naïve, trading unverifiable hopes and fears for hard cash. Under a vast cloud of spirituality we find not only churches that deliberately mislead, but also a whole smorgasbord of New Age gurus, spirit mediums, spoonbenders, televangelists, crystal healers, psychics, palmists, and prophets of all stripes. How can we draw the line between faith and fraud, between credulity and credibility? Even the most sophisticated churches, professing a high-minded theology while encouraging prayer to plaster statues, depend for their continued existence on the superstitions of the naïve.

Obviously, genuineness doesn't depend on the sincerity of the believer. Flakes and fanatics can be just as sincere as acknowledged spiritual leaders, if not more so. If all forms of belief are acceptable, how can we oppose the fakes, phonies, and callous exploiters?

These are difficult questions, which will never be decided until we are willing to accept the rational definition of what we call a soul.

Notes

1. Campbell, C.M., 13.

CANNIBALISM

Carefully ignoring the fact that their holy communion is symbolic cannibalism, taking the body of a god into one's own body to achieve a similar immortality, Christian churches have expressed much more pious horror at the idea of real cannibalism than at that of murder. Killing another human being is permissible in war, or execution, or whenever ordained by God, as so often in the Bible. But the victims are not supposed to be eaten.

This attitude is carried to extremes that transcend common sense. Unfortunates like the survivors of the famous Donner party, who escaped starvation by eating their dead companions, were viewed with revulsion rather than sympathy. But if one were starving, what sense would it make to uselessly bury several hundred pounds of edible meat?

Such attitudes contain paradoxes dating back thousands of years. There was an ancient belief that the gods themselves were cannibals, to be appeased by meals of human flesh and blood. The victims, then, would become part of the god, and share in a divine immortality. That is why mythology is full of stories about savior gods who were sacrificed by their heavenly fathers (Attis, Osiris, Dionysus, Orpheus, Baldur, etc.). At the same time, the gods demanded to be fed sacrificial victims to nourish their own bodies and maintain their immortality.

The Old Testament Yahweh used to demand the sacrifice of every firstborn creature "both of man and of beast," he said; "it is mine" (Ex. 13:2). Eventually this rule was altered, probably on account of the objections of mothers who refused to give their firstborn children to the deity. The story of Abraham and Isaac signifies the switch from child sacrifice to animal sacrifice. God then permitted animal blood to be poured out for him on his altars, instead of the blood of children as in earlier times. Ancient civilizations thus instituted holy communion feasts on the flesh of bull-gods, sacrificial lambs, consecrated pigs, and other animals.

Those who really ate the flesh of the animal victims were the priests, who were canny enough to inveigle their congregations into supporting their basically unproductive lifestyle in this manner. As long as the blood was poured out for Yahweh, the priests could eat up the meat: the origin of kosher killing. As representatives of God's mouth, the priests not only repeated his words but also took in food on his behalf.

The earliest cannibals probably excused their own consumption of human flesh by pretending that their deities ordered it so. In the Old Stone Age, it is possible that women ate some part of the bodies of dead family members, in order to bring them back to life as new children: it was the first magical reincarnation system. It seemed obvious that in order to be reborn, one had to get inside a woman's body first. The Jewish custom of naming each child after a dead ancestor seems to have arisen in this way. The cannibalistic gods, however, did not conceive children, because they were male; but they were dangerous spirits demanding placatory gifts and feedings. They were offered blood to keep them in a beneficent mood.

Throughout the ancient world there were sacred kings who embodied the gods on earth, and received worship on their behalf. When the priests decided that a king was no longer fit to rule, ready to be replaced by a more virile and ambitious rival, he could be sacrificed to his "father" god. Some kings found a way around this custom by selecting surrogate sacrificial victims–prisoners of war, servants, children, or volunteers–who enjoyed a short-term provisional kingship in purple robes and special crowns, receiving adulation from the people. Then they were killed, and became divine, while the incumbent remained on his throne.

It seems that some victims were less than willing to become gods in this manner. Prisoners chosen for sacrifice must have been more reluctant than otherwise. Even Jesus once fled into the mountains to avoid being made a sacred king (John 6:15), although this fate caught up with him later.

In the first Book of Kings we see the virility test being administered to the aged King David: he was presented with the beautiful damsel Abishag, to see if her ministrations could get him "heated." However, he couldn't complete a sexual act with her, so his rival Adonijah, who hoped to be the next king, immediately "exalted himself, saying, I will be king" (1 Kings 1:5).

When the deity was embodied in a sacred animal, the animal too was assumed to have offered itself voluntarily to the sacrifice, and was piously honored as an incarnation of the deity prior to its demise. Sometimes an entire species was considered divine, so that the flesh of all such animals was taboo *except* for the sacrificial feasts. The pig in Egypt and Palestine, the bull in Crete, the cow in India, and the ram in Colchis were such holy creatures. Animals had no control over their fate, so their willing acquiescence was always assumed. The use of animal sacrifices gradually replaced human ones, so the gods became less cannibalistic.

Even though Jesus was termed the sacrificial lamb, however, the fact remains that he was supposed to have been sacrificed as a human being, not as an animal; and under the doctrine of transubstantiation he is eaten literally as a human being, even if he looks like bread and wine. Copying the religions of Osiris, Dionysus, Attis, and other pre-Christian saviors who represented the bread and wine of the earth in their own flesh, Jesus was (and still is) symbolically cannibalized.

The term *hocus-pocus* (trickery) was used by gypsies and other pagans in mockery of its original *hoc est corpus meum* ("this is my body"), the magical incantation used by priests to transform bread wafers into cannibalized human flesh. The Catholic Church still maintains the hocus-pocus; every wafer is solemnly designated "body of Christ."

But today, now that primitive magical interpretations of human sacrifice and god-eating are revealed as offshoots of ignorance, what are we to think of a God who decreed that his son must be not only cruelly killed but also eaten? Even if the story is "only a symbol," it is a nasty one and not readily explainable as a suitable metaphor.

GNOSTICISM: A SHORT HISTORY

Gnosticism is named from the Greek *gnosis*, "knowledge," specifically referring to mystical knowledge of the doings of gods and the secrets of salvation.

The a-gnostic, by derivation, is therefore ignorant, literally a "know-nothing," or "lacking knowledge."

During the early Christian era there were many different Gnostic Christian sects, all claiming superior knowledge of God, Jesus, heaven, resurrection, death, time, and the cosmos—all oppositional and contentious. Each insisted that the true revelation was theirs alone.

Far from being the ideological monolith that we are supposed to imagine, early Christianity was even more diversified than modern Christianity, and much less tolerant. The various sects were bitterly contentious. According to Celsus, the Christians "utterly detest each other. They slander each other constantly with the vilest forms of abuse, and cannot come to any sort of agreement."[1]

These quarreling sects produced more than 200 different gospels, most of them claiming apostolic authorship. The first through fourth centuries were the grand era of pseudepigraphy, which means writings by anonymous authors who signed false names to their work. This includes the gospels now considered part of the New Testament, since they were not written by the apostles whose names they bear.

The massive book-burnings of the fourth century removed many of the so-called "Gnostic" gospels from circulation, but enough of them survived to give a clear picture of the vicious controversy among these various sects as to the meaning of salvation and the means of securing it.

It was said that wherever church councils met in an effort to hash out their differences, they customarily selected a place near a large lake or river for convenient disposal of the bodies. Traditional Christianity, as commonly understood today, gradually took shape over its first five or six centuries with many cover-ups and lies, while its Gnostic origins were suppressed "by the mass destruction of the evidence and the creation of a false history to suit the political purposes of the Roman Church. All who questioned the official history were simply persecuted out of existence until there was no one left to dispute it."[2]

Not only were early Christian sects more diverse than Christian sects today, with many different versions of the "Gnosis" of salvation; they also had numerous permutations and combinations with Neoplatonist philosophy and various pagan sacrificial-savior figures such as Osiris, Attis, Orpheus, Adonis, Hermes, Tammuz, Mithra, Heracles, and others.

Among the Christians declared heretical by the fourth-century Council of Nicea were: Arians, Basilides, Docetists, Donatists, Mandaeans, Ebionites, Manichaeans, Marcionites, Pelagians, Ophites, Nestorians, Monophysites, Meletians, Novatianists, Sabellianists, Simonians, Valentinians, and yet more.

Some of them said Jesus never existed in human form, but only as a bodiless spirit. Some said the goddess Sophia was the true mother of God and all the angels, and she would marry the Christ figure, who was not Jesus but one of the Aeonic spirits. Some revered Mary and Sophia more than God. Gnostic sources blamed God for the great flood of Genesis, but said Noah and his family were saved in the ark only by the intervention of the goddess Sophia, who opposed God, so that "by means of the sprinkling of light that proceeded from her, and through it the world was again filled with humankind."[3]

Some declared that doomsday was due to arrive at any moment, believing Jesus's promise that it would come in his own generation (Mat. 24:34, Luke 9:27). Others declared that it would not come until all human reproduction, marriage, and sexual activity could be stopped.

Some sects revered women as their founders, such as the Carpocratians who followed the teachings of Marcellina, or the Montanists whose cult was established by Sts. Prisca and Maximilla. Indeed St. Paul himself was associated with the female apostle St. Thecla, according to the Gnostic gospel entitled "The Acts of Paul and Thecla."

Some Gnostics argued that the creator-god worshiped by the Jews was "a derivative, merely instrumental power whom the Mother had created to administer the universe, but his own self-conception was far more grandiose ... He believed that he had made everything himself, but that, in reality, he had created the world because Sophia, his Mother, 'infused him with energy' and implanted into him her own ideas. Often, in these Gnostic texts, the creator is castigated for his arrogance—nearly always by a superior feminine power."[4]

A Gnostic text, *The Hypostasis of the Archons*, made Sophia the true mother of Adam, to whom she said, "Arise, Adam." And when he saw her, he said, "It is you who have given me life; you shall be called Mother of the Living, for it is you who is my mother."[5]

A similar text, *On the Origin of the World*, made Sophia the mother of Eve, who seemed to be the creator of Adam and an alternative candidate for the title of All-mother: "After the day of rest, Sophia sent Zoe ('Life'), her daughter, who is called Eve, as an instructor to raise up Adam. When Eve saw Adam cast down, she pitied him, and she said, 'Adam, live! Rise up upon the earth!' Immediately her word became a deed. For when Adam rose up, immediately he opened his eyes. When he saw her, he said, 'You will be called the Mother of the Living, because you are the one who gave me life.'"[6]

Some sects worshiped Mary Magdalene as the original foundress of the church, the true bride of Christ, and the earthly incarnation of Sophia.

Others declared that she was only a harlot, even though it was she who anointed Jesus, thus making him a Christos or "Anointed One." The Gospel of Thomas speaks of the intense jealousy of St. Peter who bitterly resented Jesus's preference for Mary.

As an example of the complexities of Gnostic tradition, let us look at the mythical, or heretical, or possibly discredited St. Valentine.

The Ides of February were long sacred to the Roman goddess Juno under her title of Juno Februata, in her springtime sexual "fever" (Latin *febris*), the time of planting. The Lupercalian festival celebrated at that time was an occasion of sexual license, aimed at enhancing the fertility of the earth.[7]

Young couples chose partners for erotic games by means of "billets"–prototypical Valentines–according to ancient customs later denounced by the church as "heathen lewdness." Yet churchmen were unable to eradicate the customs, which is one reason why Valentine became the patron saint of lovers.

A number of candidates for the title of St. Valentine have been put forward to obscure the oldest and probably most authentic, Valentinus, the third-century founder of one of the most popular Gnostic sects, which apparently incorporated some of the ancient Roman love-games.

Valentinian Christians made the Goddess Sophia the third member of the trinity, after the Horus-Isis-Osiris model of the Egyptians, and their most sacred rite took place in what they called the Bridal Chamber, where men encountered what were called "sexual angels." The Gospel of Philip explains that "The holy of holies is the Bridal Chamber. The redemption takes place in the Bridal Chamber."[8]

The writings of Valentinus say: "When you make the two one ... when you make the male and female into a single one ... then shall you enter the Kingdom." The specific nature of the Kingdom was left to the ever-fertile imagination, but it is hardly news that orgasmic and mystical experiences have always been closely related. Through the years, various female saints have claimed a mystical "marriage" with Jesus that proved to be a highly sexual turn-on; St. Theresa being a notable example.

Because of their inclusion of the divine female principle, and because of the probably orgiastic nature of their rituals, the Valentinians were declared heretics by the Roman church, even as the

February rites of "St. Valentine" were preserved against the will of the authorities.

The church might like to be rid of St. Valentine altogether, but the tradition of Valentine's day is embedded in the Ides of February throughout Western culture and doggedly resists elimination.

Some of the most popular saints in the church calendar were similarly based on Gnostic or heretical figures, or pagan deities, especially the female ones, like St. Sophia, St. Catherine, and St. Barbara. These and many others were removed from the calendar much later, when scholars' works began to leak out and reveal that the church often created its saints out of mere names, clinging to whatever customs, holy places, or deities people did not want to abandon.

I liked my own name better when I learned that St. Barbara was nothing but a Latin Christian title for the "barbarian" goddess worshiped at a tower-shrine in northern Italy. Because towers tend to attract lightning, lightning became the symbol of this goddess. Like many other pagan goddess figures, she was adopted by the Catholic church as a saint simply by rededicating her ancient shrine. The legend of her martyrdom was concocted during the seventh century CE, claiming that her pagan father killed her for taking up the Christian faith, whereupon God struck him with the goddess Barbara's own weapon, a bolt of lightning.[9] Strangely, God was often just a little too late when it came to saving the lives of his adherents.

Neither did the church become a true monolith even during the Dark Ages, despite constant efforts to identify and root out all the Gnostic opinions that were labeled heretical. Heresy was defined by the Roman church as "insubordination to clerical authority." According to church father Irenaeus, every sect must agree with the Roman church "on account of its preeminent authority."[10]

Nevertheless, many disagreed. Eastern churches seceded to become Greek and Russian orthodoxies. The Coptic churches in Egypt diverged from Rome. Jain Buddhism influenced the churches of Syria and Macedonia, while Arian Christianity continued to flourish in the Balkans, leading to the Moravians' denial of the trinity and the rise of Unitarian ideas.

At the fourth Lateran Council in 1215, Pope Innocent III "infallibly" pronounced his own church "the one universal church of the faithful, outside of which no one at all is saved." But many other churches obstinately ignored him. Not all were convinced by Rome's assertion of the doctrine of papal infallibility.

There were still diverse warring Gnostic sects, many created anew in opposition to the corruption of the clergy and its oppression of lay people in that time.

The Bogomils or Patarines rejected baptism, miracles, the eucharist, marriage, and all bodily indulgences. The Fraticelli or Spiritual Franciscans preached austerity as an antidote to the church's worldly ostentation. The Luciferians worshiped Lucifer, the "Light-Bringer," as the true giver of enlightenment who revealed the *gnosis* of good and evil to Adam and Eve. The Hussites rejected transubstantiation, and attacked the ecclesiastical simony that was rampant at the time. The Rosicrucians, Waldenses, and Knights Templar all preached mystical doctrines that contradicted the dogmas of Rome.

In the fifth century, Pope Leo the Great had approved the death penalty for what he called "erroneous beliefs."[11] In the tenth century, Pope Urban II declared that heretics must be tortured and killed. Pope Innocent III declared in the thirteenth century that everyone must obey the pope, even if what he commands is evil; and anyone whose views disagree with church dogma "must be burned without pity."

The foundation of the Inquisition was laid in the war between Rome and the Albigensian Gnostics, or Cathari, whose churches flourished in Lombardy, northern Italy, and southern France up to the thirteenth century.

In 1209 a great crusade was preached against these people, who had the temerity to criticize Rome's holy image-making as idolatry, to deny the power of the sacraments, to read the bible for themselves, and to insist that the Jehovah of the Roman church was an evil demiurge who created the world of matter only to entrap human souls.

The Albigensian Crusade, as it has been called, was one of the bloodiest chapters in a long and bloody history of holy warfare, resulting in in the extermination of large portions of the population of southern France.

When the papal legate was asked how the heretics were to be distinguished from the faithful, he replied, "Kill them all–God will know his own."[12]

Robert Briffault wrote an assessment of the far-reaching results of this crusade that bears quotation in its entirety:

> In the twelfth century, the south of France had been the most civilized land in Europe. There commerce, industry, art, science, had been far in advance of the age. The cities had won virtual self-government, were proud of their wealth and strength, jealous of their liberties, and self-sacrificing in their patriotism. The nobles, for the most part, were cultivated men, poets themselves or patrons of poetry, who had learned that their prosperity depended on the prosperity of their subjects, and that municipal liberties were a safeguard rather than a menace to the wise ruler.
> The Crusaders came, and their unfinished work was taken up and executed to the bitter end by the Inquisition. It left a ruined and impoverished country, with shattered industries and a failing commerce. The native nobles were broken by confiscation and replaced by strangers ... A people of rare gifts had been tortured, decimated, humiliated, despoiled ... The precocious civilization which had promised to lead Europe in the path of culture was gone, and to Italy was transmitted the honor of the Renaissance.[13]

Churchmen have been in the habit of describing opinions like those of the Albigensians as "a detestable pest," and "a plague" and "poison of superstitious infidelity." Abbe Vacandard wrote in the nineteenth century that the church "would have been ruined if their perfidious insinuations, which brought violent disturbance into men's minds, had prevailed." The Gnostic texts themselves sometimes indicate that the real root of their hostility was the prevalence of female figures in the early literature, such as *Thun-*

der, Perfect Mind, in which the primal feminine power described herself: "I am the first and the last. I am the honored one and the scorned one. I am the whore and the holy one. I am the wife and the virgin. I am the mother and the daughter ... I am knowledge and ignorance ... I am strength, and I am fear."[14]

Gnostic texts also spoke unashamedly the one most embarrassing truth that churchmen wanted above all else to hide: according to the Gospel of Philip, "Human beings make gods, and worship their creation. It would be more appropriate for the gods to worship human beings."[15]

It has generally been an ecclesiastical habit to describe as "violent disturbance" any doubts, questions, alternative beliefs, or criticisms of canonical doctrine. Yet the numerous, outstandingly gory crusades of entrenched religion against Gnostics and other unbelievers were certainly more violent and more disturbing than anything the Gnostics ever did; their only crime was to disagree.

> At the end of the fourth century ... in an orgy of violence, Christian literalists tore down the architectural wonders of the pagan world. They built infernal bonfires of books containing the spiritual wisdom and scientific knowledge of the ages. They subjected to grisly torture and painful death philosophers, priestesses and scientists–anyone who disagreed. ... Literalist Christianity is often credited with inspiring positive social reforms in Western society. But the truth is that the driving impetus for humanitarian change has come from humanists and non-conformists. The conservative forces of the established Churches have resisted every step towards greater compassion, from the ending of slavery to the abolition of the death penalty.[16]

"It is the proud boast of the Catholic Church that its 'monks and bishops' kept alive the light of learning throughout the Dark Age. It did, but it also kept it to itself, and for the very good reason that this light was also a means to power. For the same reason it kept it from the masses; these could neither read nor write."[17] In

391, a decree "commanded: 'Burn all books hostile to Christianity lest they cause God anger and scandalize the pious,' and in response illiterate monks destroyed thousands of years of accumulated wisdom and scientific knowledge ... Within a few decades of turning to Christianity, Rome destroyed all the wonders and achievements of antiquity."[18]

The discovery of Gnostic Gospels in such places as Nag Hammadi during the last two centuries has provided new insight into the controversies that shaped Christian traditions and the ways in which violence has been an integral part of the "religion of peace."

When Jesus said that he brought not peace but a sword (Mat. 10:34), it seems to have been a true prophecy indeed. Faith is a two-edged sword when it comes to cutting out an acceptable and defensible doctrine, and sending it forth into the world.

Oddly enough, many of the propositions put forward by Gnostic teachers are still in circulation today. Obviously no amount of warfare can completely kill heretical opinions. The Unitarians are still here, and today's Protestant sects based their theology largely upon denials of various Catholic doctrines.

Indeed, modern Catholicism itself has backed away from many of its own allegedly eternal truths, in the interest of maintaining its popularity among the enlightened, and distancing itself from the more extreme abuses that blacken its history. "The church angrily denounced the introduction of medicines, antibiotics, anesthesia, surgery, blood transfusions, birth control, transplants, in vitro fertilization and most forms of painkillers. Today the church is fighting stem-cell research, cloning technology and genetic engineering. But when cloning laboratories provide an unlimited supply of transplant tissue for dying children, and when genetic engineering cures all forms of cancer, church leaders will once again forget their initial opposition and hail these achievements as evidence of God's love for mankind."[19]

Yet there are fundamentalist elements in both Catholicism and Protestantism alike that protest violently against differing opinions, and might stand ready to mount crusades if they had enough political power to do so. The conviction that one has the only true *gnosis* in regard to resurrection and the after-life seems to be most perilous to the lives of others in the current life.

Notes

1. Freke & Gandy, TJM, 209.
2. *Ibid.*, 249.
3. Pagels, 53.
4. *Ibid.*, 57-58.
5. *Ibid.*, 31.
6. *Ibid.*, 30.
7. Wedeck, 174.
8. Freke & Gandy, TJM, 124.
9. Attwater, 57.
10. Sullivan, 115.
11. Muller, 184.
12. Campbell, O.M., 499.
13. Briffault 3, 487.
14. Pagels, 55-56.
15. *Ibid.*, 122.
16. Freke & Gandy, JLG, 46, 51.
17. Graham, 457.
18. Freke & Gandy, TJM, 245.
19. Mills, 50.

RELIGION AS THE ROOT OF SEXISM

The central premise of Christianity is that human beings are to be allowed into heaven, only because God demanded–and got–a blood sacrifice of his allegedly beloved son, to bring about redemption from their original sin, after God had formerly left all of them unsaved. The blood sacrifice was essential. The Bible says that all things are purged by blood, and "without shedding of blood is no remission" (Heb. 9:22).

St. Augustine and other fathers of the church insisted that only this blood sacrifice could have atoned for woman's original sin of disobedient apple-eating, which brought death into the world, and with which all generations were infected simply by the passage of every child through a female body. God laid his curse on Eve: "In sorrow shalt thou bear children, and thy husband shall rule over thee" (Gen. 3:16), which was interpreted as a punishment deserved by all "daughters of Eve" forever. All three major patriarchal religions still use this same text.

The early Christian father Tertullian told Everywoman that she is another Eve, the "devil's gateway," and on account of her "even the Son of God had to die."[1] So woman, rather than God, was made responsible for the death of Jesus and even for the existence of death itself. Jesus' death as atonement for original sin seems especially pointless today, when even the Catholic Church is willing to admit that the story of Eden is just a myth, because evolution actually happened.

Still, ever anxious to absolve God of the murder of his son, early Christians often blamed the Jews along with woman, calling them "Christ-killers." Throughout the centuries, churchmen pointed to the passage in Matt. 27:25, where the Jews declare their responsibility through all generations: "His blood be on us, and on our children." But this was a misinterpretation of what was actually a ritual formula repeated at all sacrificial ceremonies where a god-surrogate, human or animal, was killed. It meant that all present, and their descendants, would be "washed in the blood of the Lamb" so to speak, and redeemed.

In ancient Rome at the Taurobolium, for example, celebrants stood under a grating where the sacrificial bull was killed, and literally bathed in the divine blood, and were said to be "born again for eternity." Jesus was by no means the only human savior-god whose death was thought to redeem his followers: there were literally dozens of similar, earlier, virgin-born, miracle-working "sons of God" in the ancient world. All their myths contributed to the Judeo-Christian synthesis.

None of the others, however, were so replete with sexism. Clement of Alexandria said every woman should be filled with shame by the thought that she is a woman, and quoted Jesus' words from the Gospel According to the Egyptians: "I have come to destroy the works of the female." St. Peter's remark in the Gospel of Thomas was that "women are not worthy of life." St. Odo of Cluny said that a woman is nothing more than "a sack of dung." Andrew the Chaplain said woman is by nature inconstant, fickle, disobedient, and prone to every evil. John Scotus Erigena taught that the sinless part of humankind is embodied in man, the sinful part in woman. St. Thomas Aquinas claimed that every female is a birth-defective, imperfect male, begotten only because her father happened to be ill, weakened, or in a state of sin at the time. During the nineteenth century, Anglican churchmen declared women "intrinsically inferior in excellence, imbecile by sex and nature, inconstant in mind, and imperfect and infirm in character." The president of a leading theological seminary said "My Bible commands the subjection of women forever."[2]

According to Orestes Brownson, every woman must be subject to male control, otherwise she is "out of her element, and a social anomaly, sometimes a hideous monster, which men seldom are, except through a woman's influence."[3] Even in modern times, the Catholic Encyclopedia says "The female sex is in some respects inferior to the male sex, both as regards body and soul."⁴ Elizabeth Cady Stanton wrote: "The Church has done more to degrade woman than all other adverse influences put together ... There is nothing more pathetic in all history than the hopeless resignation of woman to the outrages she has been taught to believe are ordained of God."⁵

And those outrages certainly have been many. Wife-enslavement and wife-beating have been so prominent in Western culture that a standard symbol of "marriage" on Alsatian New Year decorations was a toy man beating a toy wife.⁶ Men were ordered from the pulpit to beat their wives, and wives to kiss the stick that beat them. A fifteenth-century ecclesiastical "Rules of Marriage" text said that a husband must scold, bully, and terrify his wife, and if this didn't work, he must "beat her soundly, for it is better to punish the body and correct the soul ... Then readily beat her ... out of charity and concern for her soul, so that the beating will redound to your credit."⁷

St. Thomas Aquinas ruled that a wife is lower than a slave, because a slave may be freed, but a wife is "in subjection" forever by natural law. A man's home was said to be his castle, and his wife's prison. Up to the middle of the twentieth century, American law upheld the "doctrine of immunity," which meant that the sanctity of the home could not be invaded to arrest a husband for assaulting his wife, because this would "destroy the peace of the home." Only in 1962 did a judge rule that there was a certain lack of peace in the home of a wife-beater.⁸ Even so, most churches still retained the bride's marriage promise to "obey."

Churches now try to de-emphasize the holocaust perpetrated against women under the Inquisition and other European witch hunts, but it is clear that many thousands were arbitrarily tortured and murdered during the five hundred years of inquisitorial domination, simply because clergymen taught that women were evil.

The Inquisition persisted for centuries because it was a highly profitable extortion racket, developed for the economic benefit of the Church.⁹ Immediate confiscation of the property of accused persons was its *raison d'etre;* the popes publicly praised this rule and noted that "the business of defending the faith languished lamentably" when confiscation was not promptly carried out.[10] There was no need to wait for a confession, though the use of torture made confession almost inevitable in any case. Many of the Inquisition's victims were women, who committed none of the crimes of which they were accused, such as consorting with devils, raising storms, causing illnesses by magic, or keeping familiar spirits in the form of dogs, cats, and other animals.

Stanton wrote: "The spirit of the Church in its contempt for women, as shown in the Scriptures, in Paul's epistles and the Pentateuch, the hatred of the fathers, manifested in their ecclesiastical canons, and in the doctrines of asceticism, celibacy, and witchcraft, destroyed man's respect for women and legalized the burning, drowning, and torturing of women … Women and their duties became objects of hatred to the Christian missionaries and of alternate fear and scorn to pious ascetics and monks. The priestess mother became something impure, her very cooking a brewing of poison, nay, her very existence a source of sin to man. Thus woman, as mother and priestess, became woman as witch."[11]

Restrictions and abuses of married women, similar to those of traditional Christian culture, are still in evidence today in many areas of Islam. The "great theologian" Abu Hamid Al-Ghazali, whom the *Encyclopedia of Islam* calls the most influential authority after Mohammed himself, agreed with Jews and Christians that Eve was the original source of all sin. Because of Eve's offense, Allah ruled that every woman must be punished in various ways in addition to bearing the "sorrow" of childbirth.

She must be separated from her parents and married to a stranger, which can be accomplished when she is still a child. She cannot divorce her husband, though he may divorce her and turn her out of his home any time, just by saying "I divorce you." He keeps the children, and he may also have up to four wives if he wishes. She must never leave his house unless accompanied by an adult male relative. She must keep her head covered, even at home. She can have no control over her person. Under shari'a law, women have a lesser share in inheritance, and cannot serve as judges or rulers.[12] They have no recourse if their husbands choose to beat, starve, rape, or mutilate them, or even kill them for the sake of "honor."

Many Muslim women have little or no formal education, and know nothing of any religion other than Islam, which preaches their "submission." Azar Nafisi notes that even when enlightened women do achieve some political powers, their progress can be arbitrarily reversed: "My youthful years had witnessed the rise of two women to the rank of cabinet minister. After the revolution, these same two women were sentenced to death for the sins of warring with God and spreading prostitution ... The minister of education and my former high school principal was put in a sack and stoned or shot to death."[13]

Religions perpetrate a great many lies. Some of their lies are harmless enough, even rather charming, like fairy tales. But two of their lies are the most vile and destructive of all human concepts. The first of these is the lie that "our" way of believing is the one capital-T Truth, and all other ways are false and of the devil. From this particular lie it is only a short step to fanatical aggression, holy war, and violence against all those who doubt "our" doctrines or call "our" god into question. The capital-T-Truthers are terrified of any doubt or scholarly examination of their beliefs, and their terror can make them collectively homicidal lunatics.

The second most destructive lie is the denigration of woman as the source of all evil: the lie that has blackened all three major patriarchal religions throughout their history, and still clings to credence today in many parts of the world. "The subjugation of women formed one of the central ideologies of Western Christianity."[14] Ranke-Heinemann says, "The history of Christianity is likewise a history of how women were silenced and deprived of their rights. And if this process no longer goes on in the Christian west, that is not thanks to, but in spite of, the church, and it certainly has not stopped in the church itself."[15] Until the lie of women's spiritual inferiority has been thoroughly disproved and abandoned, no religion deserves a hearing.

We may talk of mutual tolerance and freedom of religion as good, humane goals; but there is no freedom where women, the mothers of the race, are suppressed or abused. We should remember that up to the beginning of the twentieth century in America, "Only men could request divorces. Women could not write wills, sign contracts, or obtain loans. They had very limited property rights. Male authority was well established both within the home and in public. In most parts of the country, women could be raped or beaten by their husbands with no laws to protect them.[16]

Modern megachurches have not made much more progress toward the establishment of women's rights. Pat Robertson insisted: "I know this is painful for the ladies to hear, but if you get married, you have accepted the leadership of a man, your husband. Christ is the head of the household and the husband is the head of the wife, and that's the way it is, period."[17] The myth of Eve's guilt may be the vilest lie ever perpetrated. It deserves not tolerance but blame.

Notes

1. Bullough, 114.
2. Walker, W.E.M.S., 921-923.
3. Walker, M.M.G., 227.
4. Evans & Berent, 150.
5. Gaylor, 114, 124.
6. Miles, 270.
7. Davidson, 98-99.
8. Langley & Levy, 40.
9. Lea, 224.
10. Robbins, 173-175.
11. Walker, W.E.M.S., 1079.
12. Darwish, 83.
13. Nafisi, 262.
14. Condren, 184.
15. Ranke-Heinemann, 127.
16. Blaker, 79.
17. Dawkins, 290.

THE ISLAMIC HOLOCAUST

There is a widespread holocaust going on in the world today, with hardly any notice being taken, because it is perpetrated by a religion.

It is the holocaust perpetrated against women under Islam, a religion that claims to represent "peace," but whose name actually means "submission," particularly the submission of women to harsh lives of imprisonment, torture, rape, and frequently murders freely committed in the guise of "honor" killings.

In many areas dominated by Islam, women are deprived of basic rights to education, medical care, and personal liberty. Wives are prisoners in their homes, cannot drive cars, and must not go out without an adult male relative as escort and guard.

In some areas, young women are routinely rendered incapable of sexual pleasure for the rest of their lives by the gruesome practice of genital mutilation, which is not only physical torture but also can result in horrendous and sometimes fatal infections. It is claimed that men will not find a woman desirable unless she has been mutilated. A comparable reversed situation would hold that women would not find a man desirable unless his penis is amputated.

Under shari'a law, women have few legal rights. The testimony of a female witness in court carries less weight than that of a man. A rape victim can be punished by summary execution (to save the "honor" of the family's males) or by whippings and mutilation.

Still, according to Nicholas Kristof's book *Half the Sky*, in some African countries under Islam, up to 90 percent of all females over the age of three have been raped. Sometimes, permanent injuries are inflicted by rape with sticks or gun barrels. Men are taught from boyhood to regard the women as fair game, rather less important than domestic animals.

Young girls can be betrothed by their fathers to decades-older men, whom they neither know nor like. A girl who objects to this kind of treatment can be whipped, imprisoned, or even killed for her disobedience.

Any hint of adulterous behavior, such as speaking to a strange man, or wearing the wrong kind of clothing, or leaving home without her husband's permission, can be punished by killing, or by throwing acid in a woman's face, or by cutting off her nose, ears, or lips. A man may deprive his wife of food if she misbehaves, or divorce her and turn her out of her home simply by saying "I divorce you" three times in the presence of (male) witnesses; but a woman has no such easy access to divorce.

Brigitte Gabriel reports that: "It is shameful for an Arab woman to be seen with a male who is not a relative ... Merely creating the suspicion of being touched by another man can cost her her life. Hundreds of women and young girls are savagely butchered in the Middle East every year. Even if a young girl is raped, she still has to die because she soiled the family's reputation and honor ... Even in Jordan, under British-educated King Abdullah and his wife, Article 341 of Jordanian law justifies murder when honor is in question ... Women have no rights in Islamic societies. Women are not permitted to get an education. They are not allowed to leave the house or work without a male guardian's written approval. The Koran gives the husband the right to beat his wife."[1]

Sam Harris adds: "We live in a world in which women and girls are regularly murdered by their male relatives for perceived sexual indiscretions–ranging from merely speaking to a man without permission to falling victim of rape. ... The girl either has her throat cut, or she is doused with gasoline and set on fire, or she is shot. The jail sentences for these men, if they are prosecuted at all, are invariably short. Many are considered heroes in their communities. ... Of course, honor killing is merely one facet in that terrible kaleidoscope that is the untutored male imagination: dowry deaths and bride burnings, female infanticide, acid attacks, female genital mutilation, sexual slavery–these and other joys await unlucky women throughout the world."[2]

Cruel and Unusual Punishment, by Nonie Darwish, is perhaps the clearest analysis of shari'a law and its effects on women. Another book, *Reading Lolita in Teheran*, by Professor Azar Nafisi, demonstrates the extreme difficulties experienced by women who simply want to become educated, and are arbitrarily excluded from schools. A few meet secretly in a private home just to read books together; this is a punishable offense.

Brigitte Gabriel writes: "Arabs in the Middle East will never be able to recognize or address the real issues that are holding them back... From the moment they are born they are programmed to blame Israel and the United States for their ills. Instead of practicing self-examination to discover why a third of their men and half their women are illiterate...they turn their eyes and look for a scapegoat. This tactic is freely employed by their fundamentalist mullahs and corrupt leaders to mask the detrimental effects of corrupt values and lack of freedom."[3]

A majority of Muslim women receive no education other than a religious indoctrination into their "inferior" status, so they have no inner recourse and no hope of improving their lot. Their situation is similar to that of Christian women only a few centuries ago, when churches tortured and murdered thousands of women for alleged heresy or witchcraft, without allowing them any legal defense. Both Islam and Christianity use the same Old Testament Eden myth; both teach the guilt of Eve and the consequent sinfulness of all women.

Sam Harris refers to the "bad ideas" of places like those Islamic countries where "the totality of a child's education consists of his learning to recite from an ancient book of religious fiction. There are countries where women are denied almost every human liberty, except the liberty to breed. And yet, these same societies are quickly acquiring terrifying arsenals of advanced weaponry."[4]

Steven Pinker points out that "Little good has come from ancient tribal dogmas. All over the world, belief in the supernatural has authorized the sacrifice of people to propitiate bloodthirsty gods ... the scriptures present a God who delights in genocidal rape, slavery, and the execution of nonconformists; for millennia those writings were used to rationalize the massacre of infidels, the ownership of women, the beating of children, dominion over animals, and the persecution of heretics and homosexuals. Humanitarian reforms such as the elimination of cruel punishments and the abolition of slavery were met with fierce opposition in their time by ecclesiastical authorities. The theory that religion is a force for peace, often heard among the religious right today, does not fit the facts of history."[5]

The original suffragists in America had to abandon Biblical traditions before they could make any real progress. Someday the women of Islam will also have to revolt against their training, an eventuality that the men of Islam are taught to regard with vastly exaggerated fear, leading them to impose horrendously brutal punishments for comparatively minor infractions, such as wearing nail polish or having too-colorful clothes.

For the moment, however, the horrors perpetrated against women in the name of Allah are not made very public. Western liberal thinkers usually try to be tolerant of the beliefs of others, even when they consider such beliefs erroneous. But perhaps we are too liberal in overlooking the despair of so many women's lives under Islam. General condemnation of these sexist practices has not been aroused. Scant publicity has leaked out, considering the vast scope of the problem.

A few news stories have appeared, and a few books have been published, but most Westerners are still unaware of the extent and viciousness of Islamic sexism. They are also unaware that, because Islamic law allows polygamy and large parts of Islamic culture discourage birth control, the women can become essentially babymaking machines. Their birth rate now substantially exceeds that of non-Muslims.

In the last century the Nazi holocaust was hushed up; and, despite its irrefutable documentation, there are some even today trying to claim that it never happened. Nowadays the lifelong bondage of Muslim women is hushed up, because it is a "religious" issue, and any members of a religious sect are presumed to have voluntarily chosen the faith for themselves—even when they have done no such thing, but have been raised in the faith and have never heard of any alternative.

Even a woman raised and educated in the United States can have great difficulty in trying to escape an abusive Muslim marriage, as shown by Betty Mahmoody in *Not Without My Daughter*.

An article by Luis Granados in *The Humanist* magazine, October 2010, quotes the command of Mohammed that back-talking women must be scourged, because "women are naturally, morally, and religiously defective." Outrages against women continue to proliferate in modern times:

> In Atlanta in 2008 ... twenty-five-year-old Sandeela Kanwal was killed by her father because she was seeking a divorce from the designated husband ... When Ayaan Hirsi Ali went on a one-woman crusade to get the Dutch police simply to keep track of the number of honor killings in Holland, she was scorned for exaggerating the problem–until a pilot program in just two of the country's twenty-five regions found eleven such killings from October 2004 to May 2005. After the United States "liberated" Iraq from the secular Baath Party regime and handed it to the Shiites, there were forty-seven documented honor killings in 2006 in Basra alone. Ayman Udas was killed by her brothers in Pakistan for bringing disgrace to the family by singing on television. Harry Potter film actress Afshan Azad was attacked and nearly killed by her father and brother this summer for dating a Hindu. A four-year-old Palestinian girl who was raped by an adult was allowed to bleed to death, to preserve the family's honor.
>
> In Jordan, the Penal Code states flatly that "he who discovers his wife or one of his female relatives committing adultery and kills, wounds, or injures one of them, is exempt from any penalty." A proposal to repeal this law failed when Jordan's Islamic Action Front issued a fatwa that doing so would "destroy our Islamic, social, and family values by stripping men of their humanity."

When men's humanity appears to depend on their right to murder or mutilate wives and daughters, surely there is very little real "honor" left to them.

The situation calls for more attention from international organizations, more publicity, more outrage. It is a situation of routine inhumanity and abuse that must not continue. A religion that perpetrates such inhumanity deserves not tolerance but blame.

The most ironic aspect of the Islamic anti-woman holocaust may be that Islam itself is but a comparatively recent revision of the matricentric Goddess religion of ancient Arabia. The original cult was focused on the Ka'aba, the holy pilgrimage center of Mecca, where Al-Uzza or Al-Ilat (*i.e.*, "Goddess," the feminine form of Allah) was worshiped as a sacred black stone, covered by a veil and known as the Old Woman. A very similar black stone in Roman times represented the Phrygian goddess Cybele, variations of whose name such as Kubaba, Kuba, Kube (the "Cube") have been linguistically linked with the Ka'aba.

Mohammed's own ancestors, the tribe of Koreshites, were traditional guardians of the shrine, and called themselves *Beni Shaybah*, "Sons of the Old Woman," a title still applied to today to the priests of the Ka'aba.

> Popular tradition relates how Abraham, when he founded the Ka'aba, bought the ground from an old woman to whom it belonged. She, however, consented to part with it only on the condition that she and her descendants for all time should have the key of the place in their keeping. The tradition manifestly refers to the priestesses of Al-Uzza, and represents the male god, Abraham, as a later intruder in the sanctuary. The great goddess was worshiped in the Ka'aba in the form of a sacred stone, none other than the famous black stone which is still the most sacred object in Islam. ... Thus Muslim pilgrims from all quarters of the globe proceed to Mecca to this day chiefly with the purpose of kissing the ancient image of the great goddess of Arabia.[6]

Islamic tradition relates that Mohammed formerly prostrated himself in adoration of the goddess, reverently praising her so that one of his fellow Meccans remarked that he had finally acknowledged feminine divinity. Later interpreters claimed that Mohammed's period of goddess worship was a temporary lapse brought about by Satan.[7]

There is anthropological evidence that among nomadic tribes in early Arabia, marriage was matrilocal and inheritance was matrilineal. Men lived in the homes of their wives or mothers; divorce was initiated by wives rather than by husbands. Women were the owners of all property, such as tents–just as Native American women were the owners of their tepees–and could prevent husbands from entering by turning the entrance in another direction.[8] As in early Hebrew tribes, women were the judges and the priestesses, and motherhood was the hallmark of social power. In a Persian Gnostic text, the Omm-al-Kitab, the divine Fatima is praised as a goddess who occupies the throne of the most high, predates Mohammed and wears his crown, even though subsequent writings described her as his daughter.[9] Clearly, Islam was a later development of a formerly matriarchal religious and social system.

The intense sexism of modern Islam is typical of the cultural patterns of transition from reverence to revulsion in regard to the female principle, once men have realized that males also have a kind of life-giving power and that divine motherhood can be obliterated in favor of divine fatherhood. It takes centuries, and it involves the most extreme forms of abuse, especially rape. Islamic law tends to protect rapists, since a woman who has been raped often finds herself charged with adultery or fornication. She needs the testimony of four adult males of good repute to prove her case; otherwise, she may find herself charged with illicit sexual intercourse, while the rapist goes free.[10]

For further information on this important subject, read the following books:

Brigitte Gabriel: *Because They Hate*, and *They Must Be Stopped*.

Ayaan Hirsi Ali: *Infidel.*
Nicholas Kristof: *Half the Sky.*
Khaled Hosreini: *A Thousand Splendid Suns.*
Azar Nafisi: *Reading Lolita in Teheran.*
Betty Mahmoody: *Not Without My Daughter.*

Also, see the online publications of Robert Fisk, Middle East correspondent for *The Independent*, especially his September 7, 2010 article, "The Crimewave that Shames the World." And be ashamed. Be very ashamed.

Notes

1. Gabriel, 195-196.
2. Harris, 189.
3. Gabriel, 189.
4. Harris, 224.
5. Pinker, 675-677.
6. Briffault 3, 80.
7. de Riencourt, 193.
8. *Ibid.*, 187-190.
9. Campbell, O.M., 445.
10. Warraq, 323.

A LEARNING EXPERIENCE

A long time ago, one evening in the 1960s, I was sitting in a cafe in Basel, Switzerland, with Marie, a pretty woman who taught *Gymnastik* (aerobics). I had joined her class, and after it we went together to the cafe. Although she was a Swiss citizen, she said, she had been born and brought up in England and it felt good to her to have a conversation in English.

She had been married at the age of nineteen to a Swiss man. "It was a terrible mistake," she said. "Swiss men are sweet and kind before marriage; afterward they change completely and become brutal."

"Not all of them, surely?" I said.

"Most of them, yes. My husband left me alone every evening while he went out to the cafe to drink and play cards with his friends. When I begged him to stay home with me once in a while, he just slapped me and shoved me back into the kitchen."

I looked around the cafe where we were sitting. It was about ten o'clock, and the two of us were the only women in the place. All the other tables were occupied by groups of men drinking beer and playing cards.

"Before I was married, he said he loved me because I was different," Marie explained. "I was born to be more than just a *hausfrau*. But after we were married, he expected me to be just like his mother. I was supposed to stay home by myself, and cook and clean, and have food always ready for him whenever he decided to come home. I was very young and didn't know how to stand up to him. But I wanted to do something besides housework. I was trained to teach *Gymnastik* and I wanted to do that."

"That sounds like a good plan," I commented.

"Ha! You might think so, but my husband didn't. We had a

terrible row over it. That was the first time he beat me, but it wasn't the last. He was very religious, which I thought would make him a good husband, but it wasn't true. He told me he loved the idea that I was named after the Mother of God. I said I wasn't named after the Mother of God; I was named after my grandmother. So he slapped me, and said I was being irreverent.

"He was always reading the Bible, and he quoted St. Paul at me, to the effect that a wife should be humble and obedient, and should never open her mouth except to ask for her husband's opinion. He said God would punish me for defying his wishes, but he didn't leave it up to God; he did it himself.

"I was offered a good job, and finally the idea of extra money coming in brought him round. He took my pay every week and put it in *his* bank account, so I had no money of my own, just the allowance he gave me. Like a fool, I let him do it, hoping to keep the peace. Of course I learned that there is never any real keeping the peace with an abusive man. You know, married women don't do any banking here without their husbands' written permission. But he alternately ignored me and abused me because his friends teased him about having a wife who went out to work."

"That's dreadful!" I exclaimed. "Is it a Swiss law, or just a custom?"

"He told me it was the law," she said. "Later I found that it was outmoded, but it had recently been legal, when women were complete economic slaves as well as having no voting rights. Divorce laws discriminated against women, too. I had a terrible time getting a divorce. He threatened to kill me. He said we were still married in the eyes of God, and I was an unfaithful wife who deserved to die."

"It seems you were brave enough to stand up to him, finally."

"I wasn't brave; I was desperate. He began hitting me so much that the bruises would show in my exercise clothes. Many times I wore dark glasses to hide the black eyes. When I started to sweat, sometimes the glasses would slide down my nose and fall off." She smiled. "Some of the women in my classes knew exactly what was going on, but they never said anything. In this country, women never talk about brutal husbands. They are all afraid."

I had already met a number of Swiss women who seemed quite at ease with themselves and comfortable in their marriages. I couldn't believe they were all dissembling. "I don't think that's true of everyone," I said. "There are always some who are happy in their marriages."

"Yes, some," Marie said, dismissing them with a negligent wave of her hand as an insignificant minority. "But then many women are content to be nothing but housewives. If you want more than that, it's hard to buck the stereotype. What European men want is just the ever-attentive mother figure, with the additional comfort of sex. And believe me, *that's* supposed to be available for him any time he wants it, too. If he's too tired, there's no sex. If you're too tired, you do it anyway, or else."

"Your husband most have been unusually insensitive," I said.

"Well, it certainly was a learning experience for me," she said. "You might say I learned the hard way, after starting out all naïve and starry-eyed. Girls are taught to think marriage is God's plan for them, and then it turns out that God was really plotting to make them slaves." She brooded for a moment, twirling her glass. "Is it true," she asked, "that American husbands wash dishes, change babies, and stay home in the evenings with their families?"

"Many do," I said. "I think most American men try to be helpful around the house, especially if their wives have jobs too. The trend seems to be toward more cooperation in marriage today."

"Does your husband wash dishes?" she asked.

"Yes, he does."

"Does he change your baby's nappies?"

"Yes. In the States we call them diapers."

"And he stays home with the baby when you have to go out in the evenings?"

"Yes."

She sighed deeply. "It sounds *so* romantic," she said. For me, this put quite a new light on matters of babysitting and dishwashing. "*Romantic?*" I said. "Really?"

Marie said, "My husband would never allow me to leave him alone with the baby, not even for ten minutes. If I had to run out to the corner shop to buy some bread, I had to take the baby with me or get another woman to come in. He would just sit there and smoke his pipe in peace. If I tried to leave him for a few minutes, he would teach me a lesson by going out and leaving the baby unattended."

"He didn't think much of his child, then," I said, horrified. "How could a father be so uncaring? What if there was an accident, and the baby got hurt?"

"Then it would be my fault for leaving my child alone," Marie said. "I was the careless parent. It wasn't his responsibility. He said God gave Eve the job of having children, not Adam; and it was woman's duty to look after them. So I took the baby with me everywhere. The husbands like that, because it automatically tells other men: Private property, keep away."

"I can see why you needed a divorce."

"I wish I could find an American man to marry."

"Well," I said, "not all of them are good husband material. There are abusive husbands in America too."

"Yes, but at least people know they are bad. Here, brutal husbands think they're perfectly normal and proper and exercising their God-given rights. My husband never thought anything he did was real mistreatment. His friends agreed. To this day he thinks I was in the wrong for leaving him, even though he twice put me in hospital. European men think if a man leaves his wife, it's because she somehow failed her marital duties and he's well rid of her. If a wife leaves her husband, it's because she's a treacherous, ungrateful shrew who is in league with the devil, because she broke her sacred vows."

One of the card games came to an end. The men left their table and put on their coats. As they passed our table, one of them pointed and made a loud remark. All his buddies laughed. Marie's face went red.

"What did he say?" I asked.

"Something obscene; I wouldn't even repeat it," she answered. "You see how women are persecuted here, even by a casual remark. It is so everywhere in Europe."

"It's not unknown in the United States," I reminded her. "I've been called dirty names just passing by certain types of men. You ignore it."

"I wish I could hit them," Marie said fiercely. "If a man insults another man, he can expect to be hit. But women can never fight back."

"But you can insult them back," I suggested. "Say something nasty and belittling and let his friends laugh at *him*."

"Then I would not be a lady."

"So don't be a lady. What does being a lady do for you?"

"It's different for you," Marie said wearily. "You aren't supposed to behave like a European. You're an American, and everybody knows Americans are ... well, different. You can walk around the city in blue jeans. You can climb the mountain alone. You don't think it's daring to sit in a cafe late in the evening without a man. You have a kind husband who lets you do whatever you want."

"Marie, my husband and I are both grownups. We don't *let* each other do things, as if one had control of the other. I do what I want, and so does he, but we try to please each other, like friends."

"Ah, that's so romantic," she sighed. "So beautiful."

I wondered, was it really? Could the idea of a married couple treating each other like friends be so rare as Marie believed? I had met several charming Swiss gentlemen without suspecting that their attitudes might be sexist. On later consideration, I decided that sexist attitudes are found everywhere. It seems to be the task of women to find out what it is in the acculturization of men that makes them sexist, and change it. To judge from Marie's experience, it was tied to their ideas of God.

I don't know what ever became of Marie. I hope she eventually found a kind husband, American or otherwise, or else learned to make her own way in the world as a single woman. The one new thought that I brought away from her conversation was the idea that being friends with your spouse could be described as romantic. Somehow it hadn't seemed like quite enough–but on the other hand, maybe it was.

I knew that in one respect, Marie was wrong: the difference between her marriage and mine was not just a matter of nationality.

HOW DID FUNERALS BEGIN?

Why do people gather after a death, to talk about the deceased? Our usual rationalization for this behavior is that the bereaved family will find it a "comfort." This may be; but if so, it is a culturally learned response not grounded in nature. The original reasons for funerary customs were quite different.

We must ask, what did the most primitive humans do about their dead, perhaps a million years ago?

From the beginning, people have believed everything that happens is caused by invisible spirits with human-like mind and purpose. Despite all evidence to the contrary, many still believe this. They pray, cajole, entreat, flatter and thank supernatural beings who are always supposed to be listening. They feel that nothing in the universe occurs at random. The spirit, god, or goddess always has a reason.

A corollary to this primitive world-view is that in death, the animating spirit of a human being deserts the body and becomes one of these invisible entities, acquiring some extra-human power to make things happen. The dead are made into ghosts that, like gods, can communicate with the living, listen to entreaties, or affect events for good or ill. From the most primitive times, people have convinced themselves that the dead can hear what is said about them. So eulogies become important. The ghost requires flattery. Even today, some consider it "bad luck" to speak ill of the dead.

Often, people who believe in ghosts have viewed them as possibly malevolent or dangerous. We see this long-established tendency in the folkloric persistence of "bad" versions of the dead, such as zombies, vampires, ghouls, bogies, revenants, ambulant mummies, and other unquiet spirits.

Hence it became necessary for formal appeasement of the ghosts of those who might harbor resentments. Ceremonies of homage, praise, and propitiation of the dead became common. The ghost must be made to feel kindly toward the living.

Funerary ceremonies vary, but the basic idea of pleasing and eulogizing the dead is universal. Sacrifices were sometimes offered. Adulatory speeches were given. Exaggerated mourning behaviors were staged to convince the ghost that he/she was sorely missed. Professional mourners or "keeners" have been recently still employed in some areas, such as Ireland, just as they were in ancient Egypt. This oddly illogical custom seems to assume that the dead person forgets all about any professional mourning seen during his or her lifetime, and comes to believe in the sincerity of all the paid-for wailing, hair-pulling, garment-rending, and other carryings-on.

Another requirement may have been that the ghost should be flattered by maximum attendance at the solemnities. Huge funerary processions were staged by rich and powerful families to flaunt vast numbers of mourners–certainly not all of whom find "comfort" in such ceremonies but rather felt coerced into attending. One is reminded of the lavish funerals of mafia dons, rejoicing in hundreds of attendees, most of whom actually hated the deceased–including clergy who are paid to give the routine guarantee of his "sure and certain" admission to paradise. And, inevitably, this guarantee is given no matter how many or how heinous his crimes; God's forgiveness is almost always for sale to those who can pay.

Propitiation of especially revered ancestors became a recurrent event, celebrated on each anniversary, like a saint's day. Sometimes the ancestor morphed over time into a god or goddess, able to hear and answer the prayers of his/her descendants. The origin of our Halloween or All Hallows (All Saints' Eve) was just such an anniversary, annually honoring the spirits of all ancestral ghosts at once, to win their goodwill at the time of the harvest.

In Europe, the priestesses who officiated at such pagan funerary solemnities were later denounced by the new rival religion of the church as witches, and the ancestral ghosts they invoked were called demons. Then the pagan rites of Halloween took on the trappings of so-called "evil." But the church soon discovered that ceremonies for the dead were highly lucrative; so the clergy came to insist that only official clerical sanctions would guarantee the soul's entrance into heaven. Payment to the church became a duty of the survivors. Medieval Catholicism even increased revenues by the direct sale of "indulgences," meaning special rituals guaranteed to shorten the deceased's term in purgatory.

So it has ever been: money opens all gates, even pearly ones.

For thousands of years previous to Christianity, however, people had developed many ideas about the spirits of the dead, and had incorporated these ideas into funerary customs. Methods of disposing of the body gave rise to the very notion of the four elements–fire, air, water and earth–embraced by Greek and Roman thinkers and all their European descendants up to the eighteenth century when discovery of the real elements began. The classic four represented the only possible ways to dispose of a corpse, short of cannibalism: cremation by fire, dispersal into the air, burial at sea or in other water, and entombment in the womb of Mother Earth.

Cremation was thought to send the soul skyward along with the flames, perhaps to become a permanent spark among the stars, which were often perceived as angelic beings or immortal souls. Sun worshipers favored the use of fire, which was employed also to send sacrifices to various divinities of heavenly light. The Old Testament says sacrifices to Yahweh were often burned on the altar to send their essence skyward. Souls arising from the flames gave rise to the myth of the Phoenix, always arising reborn from the ashes of sacrifice.

Air dispersal was favored especially by the Persians, who left their dead in the topless "Towers of Silence" to be consumed by vultures and other birds. Some Native American tribes had the same idea, placing their dead on platforms in trees. The ancient Egyptian Goddess of the dead, Nekhbet, was depicted as a vulture. Romans also believed that souls of the dead could enter into the bodies of birds, which accounted for their taking of ancestral spirits' omens from bird behavior. Some believed that any flying creature could contain the soul of a deceased person. The Greek word for soul, Psyche, also means "butterfly." The name of the (Biblically-vilified) Philistine god of the dead, Beelzebub, means "Lord of the Flies" because it was thought that flies could carry souls. Some of the virgin mothers in Irish mythology conceived their children by swallowing a fly. The medieval church said good folks could be supplied with wings in heaven and become "angels," like other flying creatures.

Air was often considered the substance of spirit, since breath was what a dead body lacked. Hindus believed that a father gave a soul to a newborn child by breathing into its face. Ancient Israelites had the same idea; in Genesis, God gives Adam a soul made of "breath" or air. Being male, God couldn't make life out of the vital essence of blood, as the earlier Goddesses did. The Word, or Logos, a formation of breath, thus became his creative force.

Water burial was also popular, as we know from the famous Viking funeral. Vikings regarded the sea as the great mother of their race, and their word for death meant "a return to the womb." A burial ship was called *ludr*, a word applied equally to a boat, a coffin, and a cradle. In Egypt, the dead were said to enter the sun boat of Ra and sink with him into the western ocean. Greek philosophers said water was the *Arche*, the primary element, the womb of all life. In this they were not too far wrong. Life as we know it can exist only on a planet whose temperatures allow water to be liquid rather than a vapor or a solid, and this liquid is a major part of all living things. In antiquity, the sea was a common symbol of the universal birth-giving Goddess. The fact that blood tastes like sea water was not lost on the ancients, who also identified four "humors" of the body with the elements.

Perhaps the most common method of burial in our culture was entombment in the earth. Romans often consigned the dead to Terra Mater, Mother Earth. They wrote on tombstones, *Mater genuit, Mater recepit*, "the Mother bore me, the Mother took me back." Noting the apparent resurrection of dead plants from their seeds, the ancients likened this to rebirth from the magical earth element, which was also symbolic of living flesh. Old savior gods, such as Osiris, Dionysus and Attis, were sacrificed at the spring equinox and reborn symbolically as the new crops, their bodies and blood becoming bread and wine.

Some people described flesh as "clay." The original Hindu Adam was named Arya, "Man of Clay," the ancestor of all Aryan tribes. The biblical God also made Adam out of clay, or "dust of the ground" (Gen.2:7) imitating the ancient conception charm of pre-biblical Babylonian and Sumerian women, which was to construct a baby image out of clay, and anoint it with menstrual blood to bring it to life. Adam's creator, of course, had no female-style magic blood, so used air instead. The myth of Adam's rib being used to create Eve was based on the precedent of the Babylonian Goddess Nin-Ti, "Lady of the Rib," who used one of a mother's ribs to form her baby's bones.

Medieval Christians also believed that burial in an earthly tomb was one way to achieve resurrection. The church taught that the body would be restored intact. Saints' bodies were alleged to be fresh and undamaged even after centuries, which proved their holiness; but somehow the empirical evidence for this claim always seemed to be lacking.

Ancient Egyptians similarly believed in resurrection of the flesh, so they did their best to preserve the flesh by mummification, which we now call embalming. Though techniques differ, the purpose was the same: preserve the body as long as possible in expectation of its resurrection. A pitiful little Egyptian prayer to the savior Osiris declared that "I shall not decay, and I shall not rot, I shall not putrefy, I shall not turn into worms," reflecting the ancient belief that the dead body was actually transformed into maggots, rather than providing food for them.[1] Alas, neither mummification nor embalming really achieves the purpose. Neither mummies nor embalmed corpses look particularly viable; but their appearance has supplied ample material for horror movies.

Today's embalming industry goes to great expense (the mourners' expense, of course) to block Mother Nature's way of dealing with the dead, which is to send them back to what Lucretius called the eternal drift, and the ancient Celts called the great

Cauldron: that is, to provide food for "worms," bacteria, and other life forms. A body buried naked in the earth is ecologically useful, whereas cremation is energy-intensive and environmentally wasteful, modern burial even more so. In the natural course of things, all flesh becomes rotten meat, and then other kinds of substances, some living and some not. Nature's normal processes of decay are efficient, and waste nothing.

Then there were those malevolent spirits supposedly resurrected without their souls, such as zombies and vampires, thirsting for the blood of life that they lacked. The idea was a very old one. In Greek myth, Odysseus summoned spirits of the dead out of Hades by offering them a trench filled with sacrificial blood, which attracted the blood-hungry shades who could give oracles. Christian authorities were quite willing to support belief in vampires, viewing them as another form of the demons that they postulated to give common people the feeling of constant menace from the forces of darkness. Fathers of the church wrote learned treatises on all the various revenants and evil spirits that were supposed to threaten the living.

Fear of a ghost with a bad attitude represents the same primitive fear of the dead that instituted funerary customs in the first place. Those who had been one's enemies were naturally threatening. But the Church actually catered to human hatreds by allowing people to take sadistic comfort in contemplating the eternal suffering of their enemies in hell. St. Thomas Aquinas wrote that a clear view of hell's sufferings would be one of the greatest "pleasures" of existence in heaven. Robert Ingersoll commented:

> To compel man to desert the standard of Reason, the church does not entirely rely on the reward of eternal joy, but also holds out the threat of eternal pain. If it cannot bribe, it will frighten. But any man who believes in hell and does not go insane has the heart of a snake and the conscience of a hyena. Eternal punishment is eternal revenge, and can be inflicted only by an eternal monster.

The immortal George Carlin spoke in one of his routines about the revenge of the Christian God, who will punish your sins by sending you to "a special place, full of fire and smoke and burning and torture and anguish, where he will send you to live and suffer and burn and choke and scream and cry forever and ever 'til the end of time! ... But he loves you." As Jeremy Bentham observed back in the eighteenth century, "People who do not believe in the after-life do not fear being dead, but believers fear punishment more than they hope for bliss."[2]

Despite the obvious fact that everything that lives eventually dies, humans, wishing not to be dead, invented the concept of immortality—at least for themselves, if not for any other living creatures. Many even managed to take it literally, and many still do. Religions often insist that death is a ticket to a much happier place, a land of eternal bliss. But somehow the idea isn't quite convincing enough to make people eager to go there.

For many centuries now, people of the Western world have been convinced by their religious authorities that the deceased can be assured of a comfortable after-life only if the proper clerically sanctioned words are spoken over the corpse. The idea that any after-life may be nothing but a cultural illusion is an idea abhorrent to the church, since funerals provide significant profits. Yet Jesse Bering in *The Belief Instinct* says: "It's only through intellectual labor, and after countless millennia of thinking intuitively otherwise, that today we can arrive at the most obvious of all possible syllogisms: the mind is what the brain does; the brain stops working at death; therefore, the subjective feeling that the mind survives death is a psychological illusion operating in the brains of the living. Can the answer to the question of what happens to us after death, such a profound mystery, really be that simple?"[3]

In a way, the only reasonable support for our concept of immortality is simply memory. We can memorialize the deceased, and thus allow them to live again in our own minds if nowhere else. Soldiers who die in battle are supposed to be reassured that there will be ceremonies to "remember" them. Not that this is of any real use to the fallen heroes or their survivors—it just perpetuates the politically useful myth that war is a noble undertaking. But it puts them into a memory bank, so to speak, which gives them a kind of half-life in the minds of others.

Few of us can be genuine historic "immortals." We are not Beethoven or Shakespeare, Newton or Michelangelo. But we may be ritually remembered by way of funerals, for a while, in the minds of those who knew us and our works. For most of us, it's all we have, and it is enough.

Notes

1. Neumann, 162.
2. Stein, 56.
3. Bering, 130.

RELIGION AND WAR

Scholars say that before the rise of patriarchal religions, human beings lived fairly peaceably in kinship-based communities under matriarchs who established a more tolerant morality than the later, father-worshiping kind. It is sometimes claimed that warlike violence and hostility exist in human societies as a "natural" result of testosterone-driven aggression. However, men in earlier matrist cultures were certainly no less masculine; they were simply less violent. The determinant was not physiology but socialization: nurture, not nature.

Pre-patriarchal cultures were very indulgent of their children, giving them much physical affection and little punishment. They also tended to be permissive about physical pleasures and sexuality. There were no homosexuality taboos, no concubinage, no prostitution. The sexes had equal status although the families were matrilocal and matrilineal. Most property was owned by the women, whose life-giving magic was considered essential to fertility in general. Descent was reckoned only through mothers, among people who had not yet understood biological fatherhood. There was no caste system and no full-time military. Religion was some variant of nature worship with no strict codes, a Mother Goddess being primary and her consorts secondary. Such cultures were generally nonviolent and valued spontaneity, humor, and sensual enjoyments.[1]

Even in our own culture, where violence is presented to us every day in sports, movies, television, and even children's games, there are both men and women whose nature fends it off. Nevertheless, we do have organized and institutionalized violence that can sweep up even those who are naturally peaceable, and that can destroy huge numbers of our fellow humans. We call it war.

Religions are usually expected to support war, and usually do. As a rule, religious authorities on both sides assure their followers that God is on their side and the other side is motivated by the powers of evil. Whatever sacrifices one has to make will be welcomed by the almighty and redound to one's post-mortem credit. People are usually forbidden to doubt this. And the troops who are actively engaged in killing the enemy are usually accompanied by supportive clergy, even when the clergy claim to be dedicated to a God who says "Thou shalt not kill." It is said that there are no atheists in foxholes. But there can be no Christians, Jews or Muslims in foxholes either, if they truly believe in this particular word of God.

The clergy are supposed to minister to the spiritual needs of the troops, which frequently means absolution from any guilt they may feel about killing. God's pacifistic command is ignored–indeed, he ignored it himself just a few biblical chapters later, ordering the slaughter of many thousands of men, women, children, and animals, the total destruction of many cities, the incessant rape, looting, and other violence.

Those who are to be destroyed are always viewed as enemies of God, and "his" people are told that they must go to war and exterminate these enemies. It is never mentioned what it is exactly that God fears these enemies will do to him. And somehow, despite being allegedly almighty, God is powerless to do it for himself, and so his human minions have to do it for him. Also not mentioned (except in the Bible) are all the more attractive acquisitions that the attacks make possible: more property, loot, girls to rape, feelings of power, emotional satisfactions of a sadistic nature–although the leaders themselves may be well aware of these more practical aims even as they tell the troops that God wants them to satisfy their blood-lust.

Sam Harris points out that "most people of faith are perfectly sane, even those who commit atrocities on account of their beliefs. But what is the difference between a man who believes that God will reward him with seventy-two virgins if he kills a score of Jewish teenagers, and one who believes that creatures from Alpha Centauri are beaming him messages of world peace through his hair dryer? ... Religious unreason remains among the principal causes of armed conflict in our world. Before you can get to the end of this paragraph, another person will probably die because of what someone else believes about God. ... As long as it is acceptable for a person to believe that he knows how God wants everyone on earth to live, we will continue to murder one another on account of our myths."[2]

Charles Kimball, a Baptist minister and university professor of religious studies, writes: "More wars have been waged, more people killed, and more evil perpetrated in the name of religion than by any other institutional force in human history. The sad truth continues in our present day ... [Christianity and Islam] have a long and checkered history in which their respective adherents fought for causes declared holy ... they head the list of those who have corrupted the heart of their religion by linking it confidently to war."

Centuries ago, the Roman philosopher Seneca wrote: "Religion is regarded by the common people as true, by the wise as false, and by the rulers as useful." One reason why religious improbabilities continue to be taught as truths is that, through the ages, rulers have preferred to make useful alliances with clergy as advocates of blind faith and unquestioning obedience. As Thomas Jefferson wrote: "In every country and in every age, the priest has been hostile to liberty; he is always in alliance with the despot."[3]

Actually, religious authorities have realized in their ever-practical way that the true aim of war is profit, in which they will partake. According to General Smedley Butler, "War is a racket; possibly the oldest, easily the most profitable, surely the most vicious. Out of war a few people make huge fortunes. Nations acquire additional territory (which is promptly exploited by the few for their own benefit), and the general public shoulders the bill–a bill that renders a horrible accounting of newly placed gravestones, mangled bodies, shattered minds, broken hearts and homes, economic unstability [sic], and back-breaking taxation of the many for generations."[4]

Islam, now claiming to be a religion of peace, was promulgated by war, beginning in the seventh century. And Christianity, also claiming to be a religion of peace, was spread throughout Europe by the sword over the course of twelve centuries, during a Dark Age brought on by the church's destruction of schools and libraries, and the advocacy of bloody crusades against all dissenting tribes or nations.

Woodrow Wilson said, "Once lead people into war and they'll forget there ever was such a thing as tolerance. To fight, you must be brutal and ruthless and the spirit of ruthless brutality will enter into the very fiber of our national life, infecting Congress, the courts, the policeman on the beat, the man in the street." Wilson said this only five days before asking Congress to declare war on Germany in 1917.[5]

In recent times we have seen the triumph of despotism within Western culture as the Holocaust, and history's most extensive war so far, ruined or destroyed millions of lives. Contributing hatreds and aggressions were built up through European religion with centuries of crusades, pogroms, and persecutions, institutionalized by the Inquisition and many so-called "holy wars."

Concerning the Jews, Martin Luther wrote: "Set fire to their synagogues, destroy their houses, drive them from the country, kill them... the civil sword must be red and bloody." He claimed to be speaking for God. Similarly, Kaiser Willhelm II said, "The German people are the chosen of God. On me the spirit of God has descended. I am his sword, his weapon, his vice-regent." Hitler carried on the tradition by saying, "I am acting in the sense of the almighty creator. By warding off the Jews, I am fighting for the Lord's work." *Gott mit uns*, Hitler said: "God is with us." And so says every war leader throughout history. Pope Pius XI referred to Mussolini as "a gift from Providence." Europe's persecution of Jews was encouraged for many centuries on the specious ground that they (or their ancestors) were the killers of Christ. Somehow, religious authorities failed to notice that Christ's death sentence was originally pronounced not by the Jews but by God, as part of his peculiar filicidal plan of salvation.

Atrocities can always be excused by religion. Sadistic behaviors are excused when the victims are presumed theologically wrong.

Mark Twain said, "Man is the only animal that loves his neighbor as himself, but cuts his neighbor's throat if his theology isn't straight." As Blaise Pascal remarked, "Those who can make you believe absurdities can make you commit atrocities. Men never do evil so completely and cheerfully as when they do it from religious conviction."[6]

The underlying principle of monotheism is that only one god is right, and all others are wrong. From this it is a short step to the belief that any dissenting opinion is evil and its advocates must be eliminated from a righteous community. Hence, intolerance is intrinsic to patriarchy. The biblical god, for example, declared all other deities demonic, and that kind of exclusivity has been handed down in Western culture for two millennia. It is the basis for our dismal historical record of religious persecution and warfare.

Persecution seems to be an inevitable result of patriarchization in human societies. Dr. James DeMeo, in his book *Saharasia: The 4000 BCE Origins of Child Abuse, Sex Repression, Warfare and Social Violence in the Deserts of the Old World*, sums up the character of intensely patriarchal societies as follows: children are severely treated, with harsh physical punishments, restriction of movement, and painful initiations including genital mutilation. Sexual attitudes are highly restrictive, ascetic, and fearful. Women's freedoms are limited and their status inferior. Patrilocal and patrilineal marriages are arranged by others, and frequently imply sexual and reproductive slavery for wives and/or concubines. Heavy taboos surround menstruation, childbirth, abortion, birth control, and women's access to spiritual matters. There are full-time male clergies and military establishments, with a father god often depicted as rigid, demanding, and cruel. Pain-seeking asceticism and renunciation of sexuality tend to please him. There are tight caste systems and strict codes with sadistic punishments, which may be used as spectacles of public entertainment. Men own property, women, and children, and may regard war as their most honorable calling. Though slavery and torture are permitted and may be freely discussed, physical pleasures and sensuality are viewed with puritanical anxiety and may incur verbal taboos. We can recognize some of these characteristics in our own society, especially before the so-called age of enlightenment.

The central holy image of Christianity is that of a man dying in agony. Is that an appropriate image for children? When I was a child in Sunday school, I was told that Jesus died for my sins, and I was horrified. To be made responsible for someone else's torture was a ghastly thought for me. (I also wondered, if Jesus died to save everybody from hell, how come people were still going to hell?)

There is an undisguised sadism in Christianity's visions of hell, which serve the faithful as imaginary punishment for those who don't share their beliefs. We may talk of tolerance and goodwill toward those of other faiths, but it's merely lip service if we enjoy picturing their eternal agony for the crime of disagreeing with us. Arthur Schlesinger wrote: "Those who are convinced that they have a monopoly on the truth always feel they are saving the world when they slaughter the heretics." Why is this? Perhaps there is a secret doubt in the mind of the believer, which can only be exorcised by violence, real or imagined.

Throughout history, heretics have been accused of "ungodding God," or "robbing God of his glory," or "debasing the almighty," or "dishonoring God," or "deposing God's majesty." Such phrases seem to indicate a very vulnerable God indeed, easily belittled by mere humans. Are religious authorities here admitting, in effect, that the object of their worship is simply a verbal construct?

The fifth-century pope Leo the Great endorsed the death penalty for what he called "erroneous beliefs." The tenth-century pope Urban II said all heretics must be tortured and killed. Pope Innocent III stated that anyone whose view of God differs from that of the Catholic Church "must be burned without pity." The sixteenth-century pope Gregory XIII once congratulated the Inquisition's soldiers on their slaughter of 10,000 French Protestant "heretics." In colonial America, the laws of the Massachusetts Bay Colony ordered punishment for "worshiping any god other than the Lord God."

Such violence may be latent in a country like the United States, whose laws protect "freedom of religion." But fundamentalist rhetoric still threatens violence, in both Christianity and Islam. Muslim forces in the Middle East are told that they are fighting a holy war against the invading armies of the Great Satan. And with the exception of the Quakers, most American believers were, and are, willing to go to war and kill people whenever their rulers order them to do so.

American politicians have invented many patriotic euphemisms to encourage willing participation in the violence of war, by calling it something else: police action, armed incursion, protective reaction strikes, pacification (!) safeguarding American interests, and many "operations," such as Operation Just Cause. Nearly always, it is described as defense rather than aggression: an example of reinvention of language for political purposes. As Talleyrand said, "An important art of politicians is to find new names for institutions which under old names have become odious to the public."[7]

It is hard to get much more absolute than the slogan "My country right or wrong," which commits you to kill whomever the politicians might choose to call enemies. Once war is declared, patriotism takes on the same power as religion, and justifies any violence, without limit. As Voltaire put it, "Those who can make you believe absurdities can make you commit atrocities."[8]

Salman Rushdie put it like this: "How well, with what fatal results, religion erects totems, and how willing we are to kill for them! And when we've done it often enough, the deadening of affect that results makes it easier to do again. The problem's name is God." Even if religion never did any other harm (which is by no means evident), its carefully nurtured divisiveness has caused more human misery than anything else in all the world's cultures.

Those Americans who embrace religious pluralism face a dilemma. To what extent do we tolerate the intolerant? Should we give recognition to a faith that validates persecution or war? To what extent should we endorse our country's right to destroy and kill? Should we rebel against such national policy, or maintain a discreet silence and go on supporting it with our taxes? Should we personally renounce the right of fundamentalist religions to preach intolerance, bigotry, and their scary doctrines of damnation, to imbue their children with fantasies of eternal torment at the hands of terrifying demons?

Most citizens seem to agree with the expedient principle of "Don't make waves." Naturally, this is the safest course, but does it do any damage to our consciences? If we take the easy way out and refrain from making waves, remaining quiet in our comfortable middle ground, we must at least recognize that we are doing so.

Most of us are friendly, tolerant, good citizens, kindly neighbors. So are most people in other religious traditions. But all over the world, rulers continue to use religion to support killing and destruction, to extend their own power over their fellow humans. Will this ever change? Could we become agents of that change?

Alfred Nobel, the inventor of dynamite, said in 1892: "Perhaps my dynamite plants will put an end to war sooner than your pacifist congresses. On the day when two army corps can annihilate each other in one second, all civilized nations will recoil from war in horror."[9] Alas, what would he think of us in the era of nuclear bombs?

A nation that harbors a huge, expensive war machine must employ the machine by creating wars, and must maintain a relatively unthinking public willing to support the military behemoth when fed buzzwords like "God and Country." Hate-the-enemy propaganda is combined with promises of some kind of apotheosis—medals, adulation of heroes, elaborate honors for the dead, assurances of paradise, or sexy *houris* (in the Muslim view)—to make the young willing, or even eager, to throw away their lives for somebody else's economic benefit. It is essential that the young be trained as killing-robots, expendable and replaceable parts of the machine.

The ultimate goal of any war is not World Peace, Freedom, Democracy, Fatherland, National Defense, or any other energizing buzzword. It is always economic aggrandizement: plain and simple greed. Wars are undertaken because the leaders want to seize an economic advantage from somebody else, and the somebody else doesn't want to give it up.

"Powers that be" are perfectly content to let their constituents become intellectually lazy, naïve, ignorant and superstitious. It is not to any government's advantage to have a savvy, thoughtful, rational public. Governments want technological expertise, sure, but they don't want critical thinking to go along with it.

Fundamentalist and anti-intellectual trends in society are regarded with favor by warmakers, since war machines have no place for eggheads. The young are their fodder: the younger the better. We may despise Muslims for putting guns into the hands of thirteen-year-olds and teaching them to kill; but we seem to think it's all right for those who are just five years older. Any teenager is likely to be thrilled by being able to claim an adult-sized destructive power, and unlikely to be able to form any clear perception of his own physical vulnerability. Do not most of us, before we actually come of age, somehow believe that we can survive even the riskiest of situations?

Religion serves the military establishment in a number of important ways. Religious authorities firmly support their country's wars even if they call their deity "Prince of Peace." (After all, Jesus did say that he brought "not peace, but a sword" [Matthew 10:34] and history has proved it so.) Religion encourages childlike obedience and dependency on the father-figures represented by the chain of command, culminating in generals, national leaders, and ultimately God. Religion evokes the Big Daddy's rage against those who don't worship him correctly, and gives permission to kill them. Religion preaches unquestioning faith in the establishment, in doing what one is told without hesitation, and in the rightness of punishment for going against orders. Religion also encourages belief in an after-life to allay the natural fear of death that makes all other creatures flee from danger. Inexplicably, for many people even the fear of hell is preferable to their fear of permanent nonexistence.

Militaristic societies like the expression "There are no atheists in foxholes," though it is not a statement of fact, but an earnest wish on the part of the leaders. Atheists are not wanted in foxholes. Without Big Daddy's orders to keep them in place, they might even prefer being a live coward to being a dead hero. By all means let the troops pray while the bombs are bursting around them: if they survive, they can thank God, and if they don't, then their families can be comforted by the assurance (with appropriate crocodile tears) that it was God's will, and that is always a mystery. Nobody notices that it was the will of the government more than that of God. Nor do we notice that God professes to find human life so precious as to forbid the destruction even of an unwanted fetus, since that decision would be made by a woman and not by a government. Religion thus condones even the most obvious hypocrisy.

So the dumbing down of America is by no means deplored by all of America's leaders, religious or otherwise. Dumb means malleable. Those who don't think too much are more easily brainwashed, and perhaps more in need of an imaginary parental authority to tell them what is right (our way) and what is wrong (the other way), because it's too much trouble to figure it out for themselves. As long as there are religious differences of opinion, there will be wars; and as long as there are wars, religions will conspire to keep the populace suitably naïve, ignorant and superstitious.

What gullible, malleable puppets we all are, when it comes to propaganda! In what many claim is a "Christian" country, most people grow up learning "Thou shalt not kill"; learning empathy, being trained not to injure others–on pain of risking hell, or at least the displeasure of God. We are taught good manners, thoughtfulness, tolerance. Then along comes a war, and it's all abruptly reversed. God suddenly says thou shalt kill. Those who dare to threaten our economic comfort are all subhumans and deserve killing. What, all of them? The women and children, the innocent ones too? Yes. All of them. And the nation, mindlessly obedient, "supports the troops" that make it so.

It has been asked, what if they gave a war and no one came? But we have a vast propaganda machine standing ready to insure attendance at whatever killing spree our government fancies. We are given a plethora of reasons to reverse all the care-for-other-humans training. God may still insist on the survival of every fetus, but he has no problem with the deliberate destruction of thousands, even millions of fully developed lives. God is ever and always the compliant tool of politicians; it's no wonder that they are usually at pains to claim belief in him.

As a precept, "Thou shalt not kill" didn't even last two chapters' worth in the Bible. The Biblical God orders his chosen people to kill huge numbers of their fellow humans: ten thousand here, twenty thousand there, whole cities wiped out, every infant and suckling and animal destroyed, collectively adding up to a matter of millions. If there is any historical truth at all behind Bible mythology, it is this: the God our politicians claim to believe in is a bloodthirsty monster who not only condones war but actually commands it as the primary means of increasing temporal power. Even Hitler said that God was on his side, and so did every other war leader in the long and bloody history of Western civilization.

Andy Rooney pointed out that "The pope traditionally prays for peace every Easter and the fact that it has never had any effect whatsoever in preventing or ending a war never deters him. What goes through the pope's mind about being rejected all the time? Does God have it in for him?"[10]

Ranke-Heinemann asks, why doesn't the Catholic Church "forbid war just as emphatically as it forbids birth control? Why does Catholic morality occasionally embellish war, but never contraception, with the adjective 'just?' Doesn't the church seem to have gotten its values mixed up? If one makes a decision for children, one must also decide against war. Otherwise one is deciding for cannon fodder."[11]

Perhaps one answer is that war is profitable, and birth control is not.

The current thinking on war prevention seems to be that stockpiling weapons of world destruction will keep everybody safe because no one would dare to use them. But if the doomsday threat is a serious threat, then we must be willing to use it, which means we should actually have plans to do what we must never do: a paradox that would be silly if it were not so unimaginably dangerous.

"We all want a peaceful, warless world but we haven't the faintest idea of how to achieve it. ... We don't approve of killing, yet we train millions to kill, and if one kills sufficiently he becomes a national hero, and we are proud of him ... we are proud only because we haven't sense enough to be ashamed. We would rid the world of religious bigotry and prejudice, then passionately defend their source, religion. This, we've been told, is the one great binding force in all the world–Catholic against Protestant, Arab against Israeli, Mohammedan against Hindu. Thus instead of binding us together it makes killers of us. Throughout its history it has caused the death of untold millions."[12] Sam Harris notes that "as long as it is acceptable for a person to believe that he knows how God wants everyone on earth to live, we will continue to murder one another on account of our myths.[13]

Male religious authorities have always talked peace but waged war, for reasons that may be concealed in the very essence of patriarchal religions. Lewis Mumford says, "If anything were needed to make the magical origins of war plausible, it is the fact that war, even when disguised by seemingly hardheaded economic demands, uniformly turns into a religious performance; nothing less than a wholesale ritual sacrifice.[14] As the central agent in this sacrifice, the ruler had from the beginning an office to perform. To accumulate power, to hold power, to express power by deliberate acts of murderous destruction–this becomes the constant expression of rulership."[15]

Chris Hedges points out that "The United States has become the largest single seller of arms and munitions on the planet ... The defense industry is a virus. It destroys healthy economies ... Since the end of the Second World War, the federal government has spent more than half of its tax dollars on past, current, and future military operations ... we now have 761 military bases we maintain around the globe ... We embrace the dangerous delusion that we are on a providential mission to save the rest of the world from itself, to impose our virtues–which we see as superior–on others, and that we have a right to do this by force."[16]

Apparently we cannot imagine an end to warfare until we can, as John Lennon suggested, "Imagine no religion."

Notes

1. DeMeo, 367-368.
2. Harris, 72, 78, 134.
3. Bufe, 175.
4. *Ibid.*, 91.
5. *Ibid.*, 95.
6. Dawkins, 306; Bufe, 180.
7. Sagan, 216.
8. Dawkins, 237, 306.
9. Bufe, 93.
10. Dennet, 193.
11. Ranke-Heinemann, 292.
12. Graham, 420-421.
13. Harris, 134.
14. Condren, 199.
15. Bufe, 175.
16. Hedges, 145, 154.

ANIMALIA

In the past, it has been observed that the official magazine of the Boy Scouts of America, *Boy's Life*, carried more ads for guns than for any other consumer product. What would kids do with their guns? Pop away at squirrels, chipmunks, frogs, cats, or anything else that moved? Some day they would accompany their daddies into the woods and learn to blow away some larger animals. It was called fun. But there was more to it: we still live with the strange perverted mystique that equates red-blooded American manhood with the power to hurt and kill defenseless creatures.

Once when I was in junior high school, I came upon two Boy Scouts in the woods with a pack of matches and a captive kitten, trying to set the animal on fire. I rushed at them, screaming; they and the kitten ran away in different directions.

Of course it wasn't just "clean, reverent and brave" Boy Scouts that were linked with the destruction of animals. Western patriarchal mores have always fostered enjoyment of foxhunting, bullfights, cockfights, dog fights and other bloody spectacles involving our furry or feathered friends.

The history of patriarchal man shows much enjoyment of cruelty, not excepting his own species. People have packed picnic lunches and gathered in crowds to witness hangings, floggings, drawing and quartering, breaking on the wheel, burning at the stake, beheadings, lynchings, and other grisly punishments. Why so eager to watch painful deaths? And might that have something to do with the long-established popularity of blood-smeared crucifixion paintings?

Americans still pay money to watch two men beat each other bloody in spectacles that are available nearly every evening of the week. Sometimes the rat pack called "man" may bully, torture or rape in groups, for fun. Young army recruits learn to enjoy the idea of killing for their cause. Concentration camp guards learned to enjoy tormenting victims. Through some terrible psychological flaw or failure of moral sense, humans seem to learn sadism all too easily.

Unfortunately, the major moral message of Judeo-Christian tradition has been against the giving of sensual pleasures, not against the giving of pain. Masochistic martyrs and sadistic Inquisitors both were declared blessed; fasting, flagellation and hair shirts were commendable, while sensual comforts were frowned upon. A terribly sadistic teaching of St. Thomas Aquinas, St. Gregory the Great, St. Bernardino of Siena, and many others was that a chief pleasure of the blessed souls in heaven would be a clear view of the tortures of hell. Like their God, who demanded the torture of his son, they would be entirely without pity.

This was the same God who accepted the bloody animal sacrifices of the herdsman Abel, and rejected the vegetable offerings of the farmer Cain. This was the same God who ordered one massacre after another, decreeing death for whole towns and provinces, including men, women, children, infants and domestic animals. This was the same God who demanded the lifeblood of every firstborn child until he was persuaded to accept animal blood instead. Levirate laws said his altars must be kept dripping with blood for atonement of every sin, however small; "without shedding of blood is no remission" (Heb. 9: 22).

Pre-Christian deities frequently had animal or part-animal incarnations, like the sacred jackals, ibises, and hippos of Egypt, the elephant-headed Ganesha of India, the bear and wolf clans of northern Europe–which is one reason why Christian authorities condemned them all as demons. Innumerable thousands of "witches" were executed for harboring "demons" in the form of dogs, cats, goats, ponies, and other pets. Women who stroked or cuddled an animal were accused of committing carnal sins with demon lovers.

With such cruel visions before its mind's eye, Western patriarchal society had no place for the concept of the sacredness of all life. No Christian authority suggested that it might be considered immoral for a man to beat a chained-up dog, spur a horse with sharp spikes, or gut a steer while it was still alive. The obvious fact that animals have feelings, even if they lack souls, was not thought worthy of notice.

Too many men still think that the power to hurt or kill animals is their God-given right. Their sport of shooting wildlife is staunchly defended, sometimes on the ground that Nature would cull too-populous herds anyway, if they outgrow their food supply. It is hardly noticed that humans are the real cause of decrease in wildlife habitat, and in any case, nature allows the best and strongest to survive, which improves the breed. Humans kill the strongest first, if possible. Humans even capture wild creatures and enclose them on "shooting ranches," where men can safely destroy them at will, for "fun."

Also staunchly defended is our most precious right to drive our four-wheeled projectiles at absurd speeds on highways that create a year-round open season on all animals who might get in his way. We are so accustomed to this that we hardly notice the ragged little corpses on our roads. How many are slain in America every day by our insolent chariots?

We have a violent society that nurtures its young children on violent cartoons, while older children witness an estimated 18,000 televised killings each year, although images of sexual love and pleasure are consistently opposed by religious groups as pornographic, hence unsuitable for young eyes. Isn't it a backward sort of morality that says pain equals good and pleasure equals evil? Wouldn't we be better served by the bonobo type of morality that counsels "make love, not war"?

In their self-important notion of animal soullessness, Western theologians missed seeing the moral superiority of animals who never kill for fun, but only for food or self-defense. Yet few women could fail to understand any mammalian mother's devotion to her babies. Anyone fortunate enough to experience the true love of an animal knows that it is a rare man who can match the sensitivity, loyalty, and dedication of a good dog. Animals are certainly our superiors in sensing environmental stimuli and other kinds of perception; how dare we claim a special status among all forms of life?

Our vaunted "souls" are creations of speech. No one would dream of such a thing as a soul if we had no word for it. Patriarchal religions claim that each human self-awareness must last forever, whereas that of an animal is of no account, and may be obliterated with impunity. Yet we can treat them with a sort of cruelty that is given the curiously inappropriate label of "inhuman."

To claim immortality for one particular life form on a planet where every life form is only a temporary dynamic assemblage of cells is a triumph of denial. We are not the best of the planet's creatures, nor the highest, nor even the most successful. As a species, we have existed for less than one-fiftieth of the dinosaurs' 150 million years. In length of survival, we are greatly outclassed by dragonflies, cockroaches, sharks and horseshoe crabs. And our vaunted accomplishments of speech and technology may be well on the way to bringing our existence to an end in the not so distant future.

We can talk, and tell each other how fine and good and God-loved we are (and also how sinful and God-despised those other guys are), but that doesn't give us the right to be as destructive as we are. Animals don't befoul their nests. We befoul even the mother planet that gives us life. Animals don't attack us, unless they perceive us as a direct threat. We attack them for frivolous reasons. Animals don't enslave us; we enslave them. If animals had the technology to wipe us out, on the ground that we are pests, would they do so?

We need to abandon the foolish notion that we possess some indefinable spiritual dimension completely different from all other living things, and give more attention to learning how to live in harmony with Mother Earth's other children. We need to learn the true humility that can recognize what a small, short-lived, unimportant part of the universe we really are. The ancients said the ultimate downfall of humanity will be its hubris. Perhaps that is the truth of our being.

ENCOUNTERING THE NEW AGE

At a charity bazaar, I had set up a table for the sale of mineral and gemstone specimens. At the next table, a lady was briskly selling "metaphysical jewelry," mostly composed of tumbled stones that were either loosely wire-wrapped or mounted in cheap mass-produced settings. I listened to some of the things she was telling her customers:

"That stone vibrates at 700 cycles per second and cleanses your aura."

"That stone strengthens the heart chakra and prevents AIDS."

"That stone reverses the aging process. It has been known to cause complete remission of cancer."

"This one is carnelian, which helps tired blood and cures anemia."

"This one is malachite, which increases learning ability and enhances the brain's reasoning power."

While I was thinking that both this lady and her customers were in serious need of the alleged effect of malachite, she came over to my table with some stones that she couldn't identify.

"Can you tell me about the properties of these?" she asked.

"I'll try," I said. "That one is fluorite: calcium fluoride. It has a hardness of four, and forms cubic crystals. Fluorescence is named after it. That one is adamite, a hydrous zinc arsenate. It also fluoresces sometimes. That one is datolite, a hydrous calcium borosilicate ..."

"*Chemicals*?" she cried. "Are you saying my stones are chemicals?"

"Well, of course," I said. "All minerals are either chemical compounds or elements."

"Not *my* stones," she insisted. "They're completely natural, nothing chemical. And I know elements aren't stones; they're earth, air, fire and water."

I hadn't realized what a dirty word *chemical* is in New Age circles, nor had I heard that the ancients' four elements were returning to oust the well-over-100 elements identified by science.

"But nature is the source of chemicals," I said. "The real elements are such as oxygen, hydrogen, carbon, phosphorus, sodium, nitrogen, silicon, sulfur; all the metals. ... That four-element system goes back to the early Greeks and is quite obsolete."

"Oh, really," she said, dismissing me as a hopelessly unenlightened traditionalist. She went back to her table, and resumed her line of chatter, including some surprising interpretations of the stones I had just identified for her:

"That's fluorite, which opens the third eye and clears the sinuses."

"That's adamite, which is what you need for yeast infections and for purifying the bloodstream."

"Datolite is for grounding and balancing. Carry it in your car to prevent accidents."

As the day wore on, the New Age lady and I chatted during lulls between customers. I became increasingly bemused by her almost total ignorance about her wares. She insisted that her "black onyx" earring stones were entirely natural in color, even though I told her about the customary sugar-and-acid method of turning them black. She had not the slightest idea about general classes of minerals (silicates, carbonates, sulfides, phosphates, etc.). She confidently declared that the notorious sensitivity of turquoise to heat or light was sure proof that it was alive. I asked if she thought the light-sensitive emulsion on photographic film meant that it was alive. She didn't see the connection.

Thinking to amuse her with a classical absurdity, I told her the old myth about amethyst preventing drunkenness–from its Greek name, meaning "wine-free." She immediately took the idea to heart, and later I heard her telling a customer, "You can forget about joining AA; this stone will really work."

Once I was standing beside her as she told a shopper about a pendant which I had identified as polished obsidian. Earlier she had been calling it "black lavadorite." There is no such substance, except possibly as a mispronunciation of labradorite. "That's obsidian," she said, "which helps you see auras. It's an etheric crystal."

"Actually," I couldn't stop myself from adding, "obsidian isn't really a crystal at all, but a natural glass without a crystalline structure. You could say it's like a congealed lava."

The customer hastily put down the obsidian pendant and backed away, saying, "Well, I was looking for a real crystal." The New Age lady favored me with a glare.

As far as I could hear, not a single passer-by challenged any of my neighbor's outrageous misstatements. Some moved from her table to mine, to ask about the "properties" of my specimens. They didn't mean specific gravity, hardness, or composition; they meant the minerals' magic, psychic, or healing powers. They wanted to know which chakra was affected by which stone, which minerals attracted love or money, which were pain-killers, which could heal anything from childhood traumas to arthritis, migraine, or kidney failure. One woman wanted a mineral prescription for ovarian cysts. Another wanted to know which stone would block the "psychic attacks" of an ill-tempered ex-boyfriend. A long-haired young man solemnly asked if I had a stone that would make him levitate. I thought he was kidding. He wasn't.

I didn't diddle the customers. I tried to convey an idea of the marvelous variety of the mineral world and the fascination it holds for serious students. But few passers-by seemed to perceive any appreciable difference between the kind of information they got from me and the kind they got from my neighbor.

Presumably to help educate me, my neighbor presented me with a tract written (with at least half a dozen misspellings per page) by a woman who described herself as a "national board certified" counselor, acupuncturist, herbalist, health coach and psychic. She wrote of the expected outpouring of "Goddess energy" with a "radical reprogramming of the cellular structure and blueprint of every life-supporting substance on our planet," to be brought about in the near future by the influence of "Serius, [sic] the brightest planet in the heavens."

Well, Sirius is the brightest star in the heavens as seen from Earth, but the writer seemed unaware that a star is not a planet. She stated that "Serius" is a Grandmother Planet who "gives life to many other life-supporting planets outside our galaxy." Her information derived from "highly reliable channels working with thousands of professional people." I asked my neighbor if she had any idea what professions these people might have had. She didn't know. At least it is certain that none of them were astronomers.

Some time later I came across a catalog published by a mail-order establishment in Marshfield, Vermont, called Heaven & Earth, selling "metaphysical" jewelry by means of some highly original nomenclature.

Heaven & Earth invented new names for old minerals and proceeded to claim that they were new discoveries, each one presented with an abundance of "channeled information" concerning its properties. The proprietors included a small disclaimer to the effect that they didn't advocate the use of stones as a substitute for conventional medical care. That said, they went on to provide sixteen large, closely printed pages of medical advocacy for their stones–all of which were fairly expensive.

The mineral spurrite, well known since 1908, had been rediscovered and renamed "strombolite" by this establishment, which informed the reader that strombolite's whitish veins are "lightning strikes" that direct energy toward fortification of one's weaknesses, and create healing. Combined with another mineral, renamed "merlinite," strombolite will "bring access to the Cosmic Book of Knowledge," which is also parenthetically and mysteriously described as The Void.

Merlinite, it turns out, is nothing but drusy crystalline (misspelled "druzy crystalline") quartz, blackened by inclusions of the manganese oxide known as psilomelane. The latter is given a highly original spelling, "solalamine." Merlinite is said to bring on an instant alpha state, etheric body "alignment" [sic] along with time traveling and grounding light into one's negative energies. Heavy work for a piece of blackened quartz.

Another Heaven & Earth invention was azeztulite, which they said came from a beryllium mine and might be a beryllium silicate like phenakite (which they misspelled "phenacite"), but it is not phenakite. Its formula is not known because "the miners" haven't finished testing it yet. (Miners don't do tests for mineral species; geologists do.) Heaven & Earth described azeztulite as a mineral specially selected by a space-traveling "group soul" called the Azez, "to re-engineer the etheric pattern of its energies so that it can become a conductor or conduit for the energy of the Nameless Light."

Material shown in the catalog's color illustrations of azeztulite jewelry looked very much chips of colored glass, which might indicate a distinct lack of discrimination on the part of the Azez.

Another Heaven & Earth "discovery" was called Gel Lithium Silica or Gel Lithium Silicate, which turned out to be lepidolite, a violet-colored mica known since the late 1700s. It was said to "balance physical systems" and act as a diuretic for people suffering from excessive water retention.

Another stone, imaginatively renamed Aphrodite, is called "a welcome surprise only now entering the awareness of metaphysical stone users," though it used to be well known to mineralogists as cobaltian calcite, taking the form of microscopic pink crystals on a rock matrix. The catalog said that Aphrodite will "strongly aid the tissues of the body" and improve circulation, besides bringing success in love.

Though the proprietors of Heaven & Earth continually claim extensive empirical knowledge of minerals, they consistently misspell so many common mineralogical terms that they create a general impression of ignorance, despite the upscale nature of their expensive products. It may be unfair to single them out, since they are only typical of numerous similar establishments selling minerals and jewelry on similar pretenses. The practice of creating "new" minerals from old ones, just by renaming them, can flourish in a modern atmosphere of lenient omnicredulity and scientific illiteracy. No laws exist to control them. Their claims can be identified as questionable only by an ingrained habit of skepticism: which may be one of the most needed, if least appreciated, modes of thought.

Skepticism needs to be applied not only to crystal nonsense but also to a huge variety of topics today, including astrology, palmistry, telepathy, precognition, ghosts, Bigfoot, UFOs, ESP, telekinesis, dowsing, numerology, out-of-body experiences, scientology, Dianetics, biorhythms, the Bermuda Triangle, the Loch Ness monster, the evil eye, auras, bleeding statues, and hundreds of other traps for the gullible, many of which are continually touted on television as "true."

Appended below is a suggested glossary for the guidance of those unfamiliar with New Age terms, tongue more or less in cheek:

ABDUCTEE: One who has visited a KFO (Known Flying Object) and whose description of the event becomes more colorful with every repetition.
ALIEN: A skinny, large-headed, big-eyed personage from a KFO, whose profession involves sticking needles into the bellybuttons of abductees.
ALTERNATIVE MEDICINE: Curing disease by causing the patient to think he is cured.
AURA: A halo of color, perceptible only to eyes that can see haloes of color. As many as 29 different aural layers have been perceived by such eyes.
CHAKRA: One of seven non-anatomical locations along the spinal cord, which vitally affect the human body, in spite of not being there.
DOWSER: One who thinks forked sticks are magnetically attracted to water.
LIGHT-BODIES: What certain selected people can live in, after departing from their meat bodies, provided they will have thought all the right thoughts in their meat heads.
MEDIUM: A person neither rare nor well done, who conducts séances.

METAPHYSICS: A study of the non-existent by the non-observant.

NEW AGE: A loose collection of very old beliefs, most of them wrong.

NEW AGE NOVICE: One who thinks investigating New Age beliefs means listening to them and being amazed. Synonym: sucker.

OLD SOUL: One who has been through many past lives, and remembers them all, even though he may forget his car keys.

PALMIST: One who can hold a person's hand and see into his wallet.

PARANORMAL: The New Ager's idea of normal.

PLANE, EARTHLY: Here.

PLANE, ANOTHER: Any of many unknown places, about which New Agers know everything.

POLTERGEIST: A method employed by mischievous children to make fools of credulous adults.

POSSESSION, DEMONIC: A method of indulging in obnoxious behavior without being blamed for it.

PSYCHIC: A person skilled in the art of divining what other people want to hear said.

PSYCHOKINESIS: The art of making people believe that inanimate objects can move by themselves, when not being watched.

SCIENTIFIC PROOF: A term incomprehensible to New Agers, who nevertheless commonly use it to verify their opinions.

SÉANCE: A party, where people pay to sit around a table in the dark, hold hands, and wait to be conned.

SENSITIVE: One who has been self-trained to feel the sensations that New Age books say should be felt.

THOUGHT FORMS: Mental pictures of nonexistent things that are believed to exist because they can be mentally pictured.

UFO: Actually a KFO (Known Flying Object) because every

body knows what it looks like, and numbers of people have seen it, just as people through the ages have seen dragons, ghosts, angels, demons, vampires, elves, and fairies.

VIBRATIONS: Indeterminate units of pulsation transmitted through a variety of media such as air, flesh, bone, minerals, soil, tree bark, flooring, jewels, food, clothing, and imagination.

VITAL ENERGIES: Unidentified forms of energy–neither heat, light, kinetic, mechanical, electrochemical, potential, or any other known form of energy–that rule everything that happens, despite being unknown and undetectable.

WHERE YOUR HEAD IS AT: For New Agers, anywhere except on top of your neck.

ATLANTIS: THE EVOLUTION OF A MYTH

Many Americans, taking their information as usual from those two great American sources, television and hearsay, believe that a large continent called Atlantis once existed in the middle of the Atlantic Ocean, which took its name. They may also believe that Atlantis supported a highly advanced culture, rich in science and philosophy. But one day the whole continent sank into the sea, never to be seen again, and all its high civilization was lost.

So goes the myth. The fact is that there is no sunken continent in the Atlantic. Extensive scientific explorations of sea-bottom sediments have shown that there have been no significant geological changes for about seventy million years, whereas the oldest known human civilizations existed no more than five or six thousand years ago.

But myths are never made subject to facts or empirical proofs. The history of Atlantis is a textbook demonstration of myth-making. It begins on a single pinpoint of evidence.

That pinpoint is Plato, whose *Timaeus* and *Kritias*, written about 335 BCE, first mentioned the fabled continent beyond Gibraltar, which Plato called the Pillars of Herakles. He claimed to have heard the tale of Atlantis from Socrates, who heard it at third hand from his great-grandfather Dropides, who heard it from the legendary Athenian lawgiver Solon, who heard it from an Egyptian priest, 150 years before Socrates lived. This priest mentioned a great Athenian empire nine thousand years before his own time (that is, about 9600 BCE, when there was no Athens at all), which came into conflict with the empire of Atlantis. This latter empire was founded by the god Poseidon on a continent in the western ocean.

Perhaps the name of Atlantis was suggested to Plato by his reading of Thucydides, who spoke of an earthquake-borne tsunami that destroyed an Athenian fort on the small island of Atalanta, named for the Greek Goddess of the hunt. According to Strabo, this island had been split in two, so a ship canal could be put through its center, and the tsunami wrecked one of two ships that had been drawn up on the shore.

By the first century CE, when Philo wrote of it, "the island of Atalantes" had grown to dimensions "greater than Africa and Asia," and was submerged in a single day. But by the sixth century, the geographer Kosmas Indicopleustes presented the story as a garbled Greek version of Noah's flood. Beliefs in Atlantis were then suspended for a thousand years, and began to surface again after the discovery of the New World.

In 1553, the Spanish historian Francisco Lopez de Gomara suggested that Plato's Atlantis was America. This idea was adopted by Sir Francis Bacon in his 1624 work, *The New Atlantis*; by Buffon in the eighteenth century; and by Alexander von Humboldt in the nineteenth.

But America was not the only candidate. In 1675 the Swedish scholar Olof Rudbeck tried to demonstrate that Atlantis was Sweden, which was therefore the source of all civilization. Others have since "proved" that Atlantis was Spain, Britain, Palestine, Africa, Arabia, Mexico, Ceylon, and even the arctic regions.

The progress of Atlantis toward its present place in occultism was facilitated by Diego de Landa, Spanish bishop of Yucatan in the sixteenth century. Having confiscated and burned all the Mayan books he could seize, calling them works of the devil, the bishop later devised a way to translate the surviving few with a "Mayan alphabet" that he created by forcing the natives to invent hieroglyphic equivalents for Latin letters. He put forth the durable notion that American Indians were the lost ten tribes of Israel. This notion was also endorsed by William Penn and the New England Puritans, and later figured prominently in the Mormon mythology of Joseph Smith.

Bishop de Landa's synthetic Mayan alphabet was used by a French abbe, Charles Etienne Brasseur (1814-1874), to mistranslate one of the few remaining Mayan codices. He theorized that two letters, M and U, represented the name of the sunken continent. His compatriot, Augustus Le Plongeon (1826-1908), lived in Yucatan, dug about in the Mayan ruins, and published a book called *Queen Moo and the Egyptian Sphinx*. The title character was the queen of Atlantis, or Mu, who escaped the great deluge, went to Egypt, built the Sphinx, and became the Goddess Isis.

Le Plongeon was influenced not only by Brasseur, but also by Madame Blavatsky's works, *The Secret Doctrine* and *Isis Unveiled*. These books were published in the 1880s, having been plagiarized without credit from Wilson's translation of the *Vishnu Purana* and the Rig Veda's *Hymn of Creation*. Blavatsky merged these sources with her own imaginary *Book of Dzyan*, which she claimed was written in the dead "Senzar" language of Atlantis, revealed to her by her "mahatmas" during her trances, which also supplied her with a convenient English translation.

Perhaps the greatest popularizer of the Atlantis myth was a Minnesota congressman, Ignatius T.T. Donnelly, who wrote *Atlantis: The Antediluvian World* in 1882. He was the first to argue that an Atlantic-ocean Atlantis was the source of all civilization. He also tried to prove in other books that Shakespeare's plays were written by Francis Bacon, and that the Pleistocene Ice Age was caused by Earth's collision with a comet.

Madame Blavatsky's "astral clairvoyance" (which has been more recently renamed "channeling") was much influenced by Donnelly's work. Other Theosophical channelers later added quantities of colorful details to the initial vision. For instance, Atlantis was occupied by various subraces such as Tlavatlis, Turanians, Toltecs, Semites, and Akkadians, who raised wheat, which they originally brought from another planet, invented the banana, and powered their aircraft by the mentally directed *vril* force—a magical transit authority that was first introduced by the novelist Edward Bulwer-Lytton in his Utopian fantasy, *The Coming Race*.

In 1912, Atlantis buffs were titillated by a hoax perpetrated by Paul Schliemann, grandson of the great archaeologist Heinrich Schliemann, the discoverer of Troy. In an article published in the *New York American*, the younger Schliemann claimed to have opened his grandfather's sealed papers and an ancient vase containing artifacts, "from the King Cronos of Atlantis." Quoting freely from Donnelly and Le Plongeon, Schliemann said this material confirmed the inundation of Mu/Atlantis. He promised to reveal all in a book, which never appeared; nor were the artifacts ever seen.

Wilhelm Dorpfeld, collaborator of the elder Schliemann, testified that his colleague had never shown any interest in the Atlantis myth and that the article in the New York American was a fake. Still, to this day Atlantis enthusiasts quote Paul Schliemann and even confuse him with his grandfather.

Fourteen years later, in his old age James Churchward published his book, *The Lost Continent of Mu*, which said Mu was not the same as Atlantis, but was an Atlantean colony established on yet another huge land mass in the middle of the Pacific Ocean. He claimed to have seen "Muvian tablets" in either Mexico or India, or perhaps it was Tibet, and to have translated their unknown language by the power of his intuition.

Churchward said the continent of Atlantis floated on "great gas-filled chambers" like pontoons, which collapsed and caused its sinking.

Later writers made Atlantis a wonderland and sci-fi Utopia whose people could heal wounds instantly, and grow their crops and control the "life force" by magic words. Lewis Spence, Manly P. Hall, Rudolf Steiner and other occultists adopted Atlantis as the source of their visions, often making offhand references to it, as if it were as much a part of history as Greece or Babylon. However, their information came not from any ancient writings, pictographs, or ruins, but was "channeled" from long-dead Egyptian priests, Ascended Masters, members of the mystic White Brotherhood, and similarly exotic sources.

The famous "sleeping prophet," Edgar Cayce, was a very profitable prophet indeed. He made a fortune by diagnosing and treating thousands of illnesses in his own unique way, by sleeping with the patient's letter or picture under his pillow, whereupon he would dream a strange method for dealing with the illness, and would mail it off to the sufferer. Cayce was uneducated, but he claimed to be "spiritually advanced" because he was a reincarnated Atlantean, and so were all prominent people around the world. Cayce was able to "remember" that his Atlantean ancestors fashioned great flying-balloons out of elephant hide, and also invented other kinds of airships, submarines, telephones, elevators, telescopes, cameras, radios and television. They powered everything with giant "generator" quartz crystals. Cayce said the Atlanteans colonized all the other continents, but somehow failed to take their wondrous technology with them.

He died in 1945, after predicting that Atlantis would rise again out of the sea, off the east coast of the United States, in either 1968 or 1969.

Somehow it always turns out to be a mistake for any prophet to mention specific future dates.

Was there ever a factual basis for the Atlantis myth? There is one possibility: archaeological investigations show that in the fifteenth century BCE the island of Thera (now called Santorini), in the eastern Mediterranean, did fall into the sea. The island blew itself apart in a volcanic explosion even more violent than the famous eruption of Krakatoa in 1883. As a result of this cataclysm, tsunamis drowned the coastal cities of nearby Crete, while the rest of the land was smothered by volcanic ash. A sizeable Minoan city has been found on the island of Thera, buried under tons of volcanic debris. The catastrophe would have caused floods around all eastern Mediterranean shores, possibly contributing to flood myths, and probably marked the end of Minoan culture. This event would have been remembered in Greek legend, though by the time it reached the ears of Plato it would have been considerably garbled and hypertrophied.

Not satisfied with any such mundane explanation, however, Atlantis myth-makers continue to pile wonder upon wonder in their visions of the lost land. Edmund Harold, Frank Alper, and many others write of Mu and Atlantis with the utmost confidence in their own apparitions. "Memories" of the Atlantean colony Lemuria were published in the 1940s and 1950s in a series of pulp-magazine articles by L. Ron Hubbard, the founder of the Church of Scientology. Such "memories" present the reader with cities of crystal and glass, vast tunnels under the earth's crust, horned gods, half-human snakes, space aliens, magnetic energy domes that cover whole nations, pulsating crystals creating new life forms, and people who live for two or three thousand years. Some of these occultists claim to contact actual survivors of the Atlantean flood, who still live in "an ethereal dimension faster than the speed of light." For all their technological razzle-dazzle, the Atlanteans seem to have been guilty of hubris, which led them to tamper with forbidden laws of nature and thus arouse the ire of the supreme deity—who might have been Yahweh, or Baal, or Ahura Mazda, or perhaps even the original Poseidon.

One may well wonder why these delirious masses of science-fiction, utopianism, mythology and quackery continue to exert such widespread appeal. One answer is that genuine history and especially prehistory are seldom adequately taught in American schools. But perhaps a more telling answer is that, although Atlantis is no more historical than the Biblical Garden of Eden, it exerts much the same kind of appeal. It postulates a primal paradise—a universally recurrent theme in all mythologies—from which a fall precipitated humanity into a less perfect, less comfortable world. Deluge myths the world over have been linked with unconscious memory of the birth trauma, while myths of great and wise ancestors (like the biblical giants) are associated with infantile memories of seemingly wise and omnipotent adults.

Atlantis differs from Eden in one important respect. As a product of our own intensely technological culture, which grew out of the mindset of the Industrial Revolution, Atlantis is an abundantly technological Eden. Its fabled wisdom is not scriptural fiction but science fiction. Even though occultists often express disillusionment with technology per se, they still clothe in gaudy trappings of misunderstood, misinterpreted, and popularized science their need to believe in a primal perfection. So the Atlanteans are seen as scientific wizards destroyed by their own arrogance, a fate that many fear for our own civilization. Atlanteans may be ourselves, viewed through the distorted mirrors of myth by people who fear reality and fail to recognize fantasy.

The Atlantis archetype has all the elements common to the most durable myths: moral precept and warning, the drama of catastrophe, the aura but not the discipline of hard knowledge, the ever-repeated fall from paradise, another version of the Deluge, and that grand old comforter of the ignorant, the story of past intellectual greatness that built its towers too high, encroached on the territory of the gods, and consequently suffered destruction.

Atlantis mythology also caters to the human love of mystical elitism: the sense of being among the chosen, of having secret information and deep intuitions not granted to the common herd. Atlantis enthusiasts are almost invariably self-declared Atlanteans themselves, having access to its exotic memories and its dreams of glory. They are willing to share their dreams with the *hoi polloi*, for a price of course. And there are always many who willingly believe and follow any persuasive charlatan who comes along with a vision that relieves the ordinariness of life, the more bizarre the better.

This is the basic story behind all myths. We repeat them, we enjoy them, we tell them to our children, we make them part of our culture. And, more often than we should, we believe them.

A CONVERSATIONAL INTERVIEW

Echoing a cliché that has resounded through centuries, he said: "People need to believe in a religion because it comforts them. People don't want to face the unknown."

She said, "But they face it anyway. The universe is full of unknowns. Most of what is known to scientists is still unknown to the general public; and scientists are the first to admit that science knows only a little, compared to what remains to be discovered. Not knowing is our usual state of existence. But if people want less of the unknown, why don't they make more effort to learn what is known?"

"Because study is hard," he said. "People want simple, understandable answers and reassurances. God is there, everything's okay, you don't have to concentrate. That's comfort."

"That's infantile," she snorted. "Children may need that, but adults shouldn't. How can it be comforting to believe what you know, at some level, is improbable or impossible? It's a thin crust over an abyss."

"Maybe so," he said, "but most people want to be infantile in that way. They'd rather call the unknown God and then assume that because it has a name, they know it."

"There is a paradox," she replied. "Theologians say God is unknowable, then go on to explain in great detail what they profess to know about him. If you equate God with the unknown, then you worship something you know nothing about. How could you know it wants to be worshiped? Or even if it has wants at all, or any kind of intelligence in the human sense? Even sillier, how could you think the unknown has such a colossal ego as to require all those perpetual praises and adulations that are constantly addressed to God? The whole concept of 'unknown god' makes no sense."

"Well, does it make any more sense to call it Goddess?"

"Actually, yes, if you understand that Goddess is not a transcendent reality, like God is supposed to be, but a metaphor, symbolizing Earth, nature, the biological and nurturant power that *is* predominantly female in the natural world. But I wouldn't envision Goddess as a remedy for my own ignorance.

"Curiosity is a fine thing when it impels us to find out more about our world, or ourselves. Curiosity is important. We need to look for real answers, not let our curiosity be slaked by improbable stories made up by people who had no genuine knowledge. Legends, myths, and fairy tales are entertainment, not enlightenment. We can enjoy science fiction without assuming it to be science fact. Fiction is part of our lives but it should never be put forth as fact."

"Don't you think fiction can give insight into facts—about human nature, for instance?" he asked.

"Of course it can, and often does," she said. "But that's not the same as presenting Biblical myths as literal history, forcing people to profess belief in obvious impossibilities. That's demeaning to the human mind. One should be free to criticize and reject explanations that contradict the proven laws of nature. It also demeans even the traditional concept of God, who is assumed to have given humans curiosity, an intelligent mind, and the capacity to learn, and then forbade their use."

"Shouldn't human beings be free to choose the impossible explanations as well, if they want to?"

"Yes, but unfortunately in matters of religion it's not a free choice. It is so pervasive a part of our culture that most people grow up taking it for granted, and in adulthood they can't think it through. Remember Ignatius Loyola is alleged to have said, 'Give me a child before the age of seven, and I will have him for life.' It works. Once people accept the improbable, it takes on the same aura of 'comfort' that they associate with childhood generally. Belief in God is the adult version of belief in Santa Claus, only without the eventual letting-go.

"As a child, I was troubled by the nagging suspicion that Santa Claus didn't make sense. How could he possibly come down every chimney in the world and leave toys for every child, all in one night? And if he was fat, as shown, how could he fit through any chimney in the first place? How could one sleigh hold all those trillions of toys? How could reindeer fly?

"I was greatly comforted by the eventual revelation that Santa wasn't an alien supernatural being after all, but a symbolic expression of my parents' love, which I could trust. Transition from God to Goddess is something like that."

"But especially if human relationships aren't satisfactory," he said, "people want more meaning in their lives than just biological and sociological conditions."

"Meaning and belief are not the same," she answered. "There are lots of good, rational ways to give 'meaning' to one's life: successfully raising children, helping others, teaching, healing, creating art, meeting personal goals, acquiring what you desire: love, money, power. Those are meanings. Mere existence, all by itself, doesn't mean anything; it simply *is*."

"But that's the point," he said. "Is-ness isn't enough. People want their mere is-ness to mean something."

"What kind of something?"

"I don't know. That's the unknown that needs faith."

"I hardly think the human race is justified in thinking that its mere existence has a transcendent meaning, other than the obvious fact that it is over-proliferating itself and causing vast extinctions of other species. When the inevitable has happened and we have finally brought about our own extinction, some species will survive and go on to evolve in a different, humanless world–maybe even develop a newer and higher intelligence in a few million years. Life forms will continue to evolve on this planet until the sun stops radiating heat and light, and there is no more liquid water. But our existence here as a species is very recent, very temporary and provisional, compared to most of geologic time. Furthermore, compared to most other species, we seem to be eating ourselves out of house and home at a very fast rate. Can that be called meaning?"

"No," he said, "but I think you have a very pessimistic view."

"Not pessimistic, just realistic. We have no reason to believe ourselves intrinsically different from other species just because we have managed to develop languages and technologies. Language is often a problem as well as an advantage: for instance, we create words for things that don't exist, then use the words themselves as proof of existence. Moreover, we have become our own worst enemies. Unlike the majority of other creatures, we kill our own kind with great enthusiasm. Species come and go. Each may change its environment for better or worse, from their own point of view. Nature doesn't care, either way. The life force–or Goddess, if you will–goes on until conditions no longer support the process. Where is there any transcendent meaning in that?"

"Do you see nothing good in human existence?" he asked.

"Of course, from the human viewpoint there is much good in our existence, even when it's bad for other creatures. Much of what we create may be enjoyable, useful, or harmless, though that's a moot point.

"Cutting down trees to build a house is good for us but bad for the birds, squirrels, and insects whose homes we have destroyed. If a man likes to go out in the woods and shoot deer, are the deer having a good time? Every day we kill millions of animals for food, for clothing, or for nothing just because they get in the way of our cars. Naturally we think it is good to have food, even if we have to kill to get it. We want to travel, even if it pollutes our environment and piles up roadkill. Our is-ness hurts the rest of the world largely because there are too many of us. When the human population of the earth was much smaller, our predatory ways didn't upset the balance of nature to such an extent. If there were a god planning the running of this whole planet, do you think he should have arranged such an imbalance?"

"Theologians are always pointing out that it's folly to try to comprehend the ways of God from the viewpoint of human logic."

"That's natural enough," she said, "because logic can't support their premises. They have a vested interest in advising faith as a substitute for logic. But I think that's a profound mistake. The only thing we really have going for us, as a species, is our ability to reason. Today we need that ability more than ever. It's faith that told us we had the right to exploit and destroy other creatures. It's faith that told us women were born to be enslaved by men. It's faith that told us we were virtuous when we went to war, to kill multitudes. It's faith that teaches us to be irrational. It's faith that loads us with guilt for being sexual creatures, that denies the inevitability of our death, that fosters interracial hatreds, and that demands too many of our dwindling resources that could be more sensibly utilized.

"It's faith that encourages us toward literal belief in angels, devils, ghosts, vampires, past lives, resurrection of the dead, chimeras, sorcery, witchcraft, divination, miracles, necromancy, channeling, vibrational healing, levitation, snake oil, space beings, and all the other supernatural gewgaws that we love to contemplate. We ought to be able to think about things rationally before committing to a belief in them; but every theologian knows that faith has to be instilled *before* a child matures enough to think rationally. That way, rationality is forever closed off in the matters that demand faith."

"Rationality is also closed off in matters of love, sympathy, sorrow, anger, and most other emotions," he said, "yet they certainly exist. Are you trying to deny everything that isn't logical?"

"No, of course not," she said. "But sane people learn to direct their emotions to their direct causes, not to the unknown. We have no reason to believe that anything in the universe, except other humans and a few domesticated animals, will respond to human emotions. God is not demonstrable except as metaphor, and I would just as soon call that Goddess because of the huge collection of destructive consequences brought about by the concept of God."

"Would you call your Goddess concept a faith, then?" he asked.

"No. I'm not so crude as to propose any literal belief in a Big Mama sitting up in the clouds, or under a mountain. I'd call it, perhaps, a work of art, or a poem, or just an idea, remembering that all ideas are human products. We must not pretend that symbols are facts, no matter how precisely descriptive they seem to be. I like the word Goddess because it's fresh in the modern context, and has far less mythological baggage, compared to the word God. It hints at a Mother Nature, which is certainly the true origin of us all. Some people are so simplistic as to describe atheism as a religion, thus proving that they don't even know the meaning of the word religion. It means believing in something–anything–that is supernatural and should be worshiped. To the atheist, there is nothing supernatural, there is nothing to be worshiped, and humans must take care of each other because no superhuman daddy is going to do it for them."

"So you're perfectly comfortable with the word 'unknown,' leaving everything not-yet-studied in a limbo of darkness?"

She smiled. "Of course. How could you be frightened of anything you know nothing about? I don't insist on undefined transcendent meanings. As far as we can tell for certain, life just exists, and we are far too small and ignorant to assume that our ideas of meaning or purpose have any cosmic significance. This is the world's most egotistic assumption on the part of little creatures with enormous egos. We only need to live our lives as usefully as possible, do our best and enjoy it when we can, and certainly not to look forward to either eternal agony in a hell of the god's own devising, or eternal bliss of which we have no real idea, because it has never been exactly described."

"I see your point," he said. "But there are millions of people who are going to be terribly disappointed after they're dead, to find out that they have been conned."

She laughed. "Fortunately for them," she said, "they'll never know."

BEAUTY

An intensely patriarchal society tends to cripple women with many paradoxes. For example, when men control all sources of money, women can't live without male support, which they must win by "feminine wiles" because they have no other power. At the same time, feminine wiles are viewed as sly and underhanded, if not devilish. Sexuality is women's sole permitted economic tool, whether as wives, mistresses or prostitutes; and sex is considered a necessary evil, the carrier of original sin, an eternal snare for men, who pretend to be helpless in its grip.

"A man's right to confer judgment on any woman's beauty while remaining himself unjudged is beyond scrutiny because it is thought of as God-given."[1] Women must make themselves attractive to the opposite sex, while men in general are thought to be less coerced.

In regard to the sinfulness of sex, men never seem to inquire, if God meant to forbid it, why would he have made it enjoyable? Does God then deliberately toy with humans, loading them with temptations and then watching them succumb, so he can have the cruel satisfaction of punishing them? But the alleged problem of sexual attraction is never blamed on God; it is blamed on women, who are actually its victims more often than not.

It is perhaps notable that women's fashions tend to make them even more helpless, perhaps to insure that they can't run away if attacked. For many centuries, upper-class Chinese women had their feet brutally deformed by binding, starting at the age of five. The operation caused years of almost unendurable suffering and sometimes fatal infections or other complications, but when successful it crippled women so they could hardly walk and it was impossible for them to run at all. Men were taught to be highly sexually stimulated by the spectacle of those pitiful stubs of feet at the ends of women's legs.

In my freshman year of college, I attended a prom weekend at the Naval Academy in Annapolis, Maryland. I took just one pair of shoes: the then-popular "baby doll" pumps with four-inch spike heels and paper-thin soles. After a full weekend of dances and sightseeing walks on the cobblestoned streets of Annapolis, my ankles were puffed like sausages, and the balls of my feet were purple with broken blood vessels. It took more than a week for me to walk again without hobbling. I threw those shoes away and never again wore high heels; but this experience made me acutely conscious of the agonies that those Chinese women must have suffered, not to mention generations of European women who stuffed their feet into too-small shoes because tiny feet were admired by men, with results like bunions, corns, and bone spurs. But spike heels have not gone out of fashion even today; they are still considered "sexy," perhaps because men subconsciously realize that no woman wearing them can escape by running.

The tiny waist was another "sexy" characteristic that became popular enough to put women into breath-stopping corsets, which made them prone to fainting, and huge multiple skirts, in which no one could ever hope to run. Under the layers of skirts, however, their genitals were uncovered, so in theory they could offer little impediment to rape. When the "Bloomer Girls" first introduced a version of underpants, they were ridiculed and called immoral.

It is interesting that women were expected to conform to minority standards in order to be thought beautiful. In former times when food was often scarce and people tended to be skinny, fat meant affluence and fertility, and was considered a prerequisite for female beauty, as demonstrated by the Rubens-type nudes and the pleasingly plump Goddess figures of antiquity. Nowadays, food is plentiful and so fat is a fashion crime. Modern women often go to extreme lengths to conform to fashion standards of thinness: annual thousands of expensive tummy tucks, surgical stomach ligatures, extreme diets, and anorexia are among the results.

Young girls are indoctrinated into impossible beauty standards for their adult bodies by dolls such as Barbie and her numerous imitators, allegedly "teen figures" with tiny waists, large breasts without nipples, disproportionately long thin legs, and feet almost as small as those of the crippled Chinese women. A real woman with the proportions of Barbie would have a 38-inch bust, an 18-inch waist, legs almost twice as long as her torso, and about the same shoe size as a 4-year-old child. How many Barbie-admiring girls have grown up to acquire breast implants, face lifts, skin peels, nose jobs, and other unnecessary surgeries that cater to the billons-of-dollars-a-year beauty industry?

Then there are the cosmetics, among the most profitable of commercial products. The cosmetic industry is a massive con, "a sweetly disguised form of commercial robbery" with profit margins of over 50 percent on a revenues of 20 billion dollars worldwide.[2] Cosmetics are considered *de rigueur* for every woman regardless of age or social status. Our culture has little girls yearning to put on lipstick when they are hardly out of diapers, teenagers snubbing their contemporaries who neglect to paint their eyelids with shadow, and old women caking their wrinkles with pasty makeup in a fruitless attempt to look younger. Native American women, by contrast, used to look forward to their first acquisition of wrinkles, because wrinkles stood for the onset of cronehood as the season of their mature wisdom.

How much time does the average American woman waste in doing her makeup before she feels able to go out and face strangers on the street? The cosmetics industry profits enormously from the feelings of inferiority imposed on women in regard to their looks. Even female characters in sci-fi movies, presumably from a far more enlightened future time, never appear without eye shadow and lipstick.

Popular women's magazines and other publications are used to set the standards of fashion as well as providing outlets for advertising. During World War II, when female labor was needed in factories, stories and articles in magazines glorified a muscular and competent Rosie the Riveter and touted the virtues of women who went to work for the war effort, to "free" (a euphemism indeed) men for the battlefield.

Later, when the surviving heroes returned home, suddenly the magazines were full of the joys of domesticity and the defeminizing effects of outside careers for women. What real woman, they asked, would want to trade husband-and-children for competition with men in the tough cutthroat world of business? Such a woman would be a dragon, a harpy, a robot, or a dried-up prune devoid of sexual attractiveness. She would deserve to be unhappy.

Happiness meant becoming the lifelong unpaid servant of a man, and the devoted mother of "his" children. The old, slightly contemptuous term "housewife" was suddenly transformed into a more euphemistic "homemaker," a combination of cook, waitress, nursemaid, mistress, companion, laundress, chauffeur, hostess, decorator, housekeeper, valet, messenger, and general assistant to a husband. A "working mother," on the other hand, was one who left her home unattended and went elsewhere to earn some money, the implication being that she somehow failed in her more natural duties.

Women's magazines seldom encouraged any kind of independent thought among their readers, but devoted their pages to cookie-cutter stereotypes that often gave women impossibly frivolous views of themselves. Women's minds were presumed to focus on narrow and personal subjects; they could not be interested in history, science, business, philosophy, or "good" literature full of five-syllable words.

The happy housewife was viewed as a good manager and a thrifty budget-keeper, but also a bit of a charming airhead who couldn't quite comprehend a checkbook. Wifely extravagance was not entirely reprehensible if it created insatiable desires for consumer goods; after all, the magazines served the advertisers, not the readers. Also contradictory is the fact that such magazines even today feature at least one weight-loss article per issue, along with recipes for Chocolate Caramel Pecan Nougat Pie and Mocha Ice Cream Fudge Cake.

Even more contradictory are the articles on clothes, hairstyles, and makeup, which change every year to keep the consumer buying. Naturally, the advertisers would have no use for a woman benighted enough to ignore fashion and eschew the hair salon.

Makeup is the subject of at least one article per issue, its colors and applications being constantly revised. The cumulative message is that your normal unretouched appearance is never acceptable. But perhaps the silliest contradiction of all was the glorification of the Natural Look, which was to be artificially achieved.

It is said over and over that women must "fear" their tiny facial lines, their first gray hairs, the appearance of upper-arm flab, and other indications of aging. Men may grow older, but women should try to stop the life cycle about the age of thirty. Menopause is usually regarded as pathological. In addition to obsessive daily self-criticism in matters of appearance, women are also supposed to constantly assess their own sexual allure, lovability quotient, and psychological fitness according to standards provided by a wide assortment of experts in the business of telling women what's wrong with them. The total message of patriarchal society to women, delivered in dozens of different ways in many different contexts, is "you're not good enough the way you are; you must become better, and you need us to make it so."

On consideration, women's magazines serve women badly. Their slick appearance, eye-catching colors, and saccharine format lure women into the implication that women's world is always frivolous and unimportant compared to the serious doings of men, and woman must defer to men's tastes if they are to consider themselves worthy of attention. Most of all, they are reminded that hefty amounts of money, time, and effort must be spent on trying to make themselves beautiful.

Of course human beings have always done strange things to their bodies in order to conform to cultural standards of appearance: scarification, piercings, neck elongations, tattoos, the strange enlargements of earlobes and lips practiced by certain African tribes. We never tire of messing with our looks. But patriarchal societies are notorious for insisting that women, much more than men, must look different from the way nature intends them to look; they must "improve" in order to attract the men on whom their livelihood depends, even when the so-called improvement is a deformity, and perhaps especially when it causes unnecessary suffering. Patriarchies prefer that women be unnatural, unsuccessful, uneducated, undefended, and unresisting–but never unattractive. After all, God put them here to seduce men into sin.

Notes

1. Wolf, 87.
2. *Ibid.*, 98.

WOMEN AND WAR

There is an instinctive behavior pattern in all mammalian females that makes them fiercely protective of their young. An animal mother will immediately attack–and if possible, kill–any creature that threatens her offspring. Among humans, who can obey their culture more than their instincts, this behavior pattern may be modified to allow mothers to passively allow their children's lives to be taken for the sake of a government, a religion, a hierarchy, or even an abstract idea of honor.

Though mothers usually have a profound conviction that anything potentially destructive to their children's wellbeing is a moral evil, they can be induced to support a war effort dedicated to the endangerment of their own children and also those of other mothers, who happen to live in the realm of the enemy. Most women do not control the cultural symbols that convert enemy people into a sort of vermin to be exterminated. In wartime, women are forbidden even to pity the innocent victims of their own country's attacks.

Warriors throughout history have been taught that the women of both sides might be sexually available: the enemy's women through rape, the friendly women through awe and admiration of the "hero." Though history shows that women are often exposed to danger in war, until quite recently women are not usually sent into battle. Part of the reason may be that fewer women are susceptible to the kind of indoctrination that makes good soldiers.

Patriarchal morality takes little note of considerations of empathy for war's victims. Male priesthoods put into the mouths of their gods some high-sounding cant about peace and brotherhood, but any god can become a militant sword-waving Mars at the drop of a helmet. This is especially evident in history, where wars have been a significant source of the treasures amassed by clergy. Women can hardly trust male-dominated religions to bring permanent peace to the world, for God or Allah will string them along, endlessly promising peace but able to preach death to the (infidels, communists, fascists, terrorists, atheists, imperialists, rebels, or any ethnic or national group of their choice). Those on the Other Side are always pronounced evil enough to deserve extermination *as a group*. Meanwhile, the women at home are encouraged to think of the armies as their protectors and defenders, despite the fact that war, second only to overpopulation, is the most threatening menace to all the world's children today.

Women should not allow their maternal protectiveness to be twisted into aiding oppression. They should be able to work effectively for a universal understanding and cooperation, to allow the world's children to live without fear. Perhaps the image of the ancient Mother Goddess should be brought back into focus, to assert women's basic morality and make it stick.

In the early cultures that postulated a Great Mother/Creatress, there was a sense of human interrelatedness. When patriarchal gods came along, the idea of universal blood-brotherhood and -sisterhood retained propaganda value but lost its heart. The militaristic empires could hardly talk of universal brotherhood while sending armies out to kill the brothers. Instead, wars became "holy wars" and killing was an act of obedience to God's will. No one seemed to notice that if almighty God wanted a particular group of people dead, he could easily do it himself in minutes (as in the Sodom and Gomorrah incident) without having to depend on one group of "his" children to murder another group of "his" children.

The Father God's all-too-successful suppression of the Mother Goddess was the historical tragedy that engendered full-scale patriarchy. Ever since, "man's" vaunted progress has incorporated ever more sophisticated methods of killing ever larger numbers of people. War alone has killed at least a hundred million since the turn of the twentieth century CE. If humans could see themselves as children of one universal Mother, as they once did, then members of the human family might become somewhat more brotherly and sisterly. But if it doesn't happen fairly soon, we could very well cause the destruction of our entire species, which for other life forms on this planet might constitute "good riddance."

Modern leaders have achieved an ultimate power, as they understand power: the capability of total destruction. Can hubris aspire any higher? We sorely need a new image of an all-wise Mother who can take dangerous toys away from boys before they hurt themselves. Where is such an image to be found? Women, not necessarily committed to the slaughter of each other's children, might call male establishments to account for their crimes against posterity. Women must cease to feel intimidated by the male God into silence, obedience, and false guilt. The dismal history of patriarchal ethics shows that they cannot be depended upon to do the right thing.

Feminist scholars have written many excellent books, but patriarchy feeds on women's ignorance of them. Television, meanwhile, has male fundamentalist preachers pouring forth incessant propaganda, while "entertainment" often means dramas where women are belittled, raped, murdered, or otherwise abused, all being presented so that commercials may accomplish their sales pitch.

We need to learn that love is not a right to be demanded, but a privilege to be earned. We need to adjust the priorities, to subordinate material wealth and commercial innovation to the needs of the environment and the future. Some men are quite aware of this already, but it has not been formalized as yet. It is a work in progress, and for the sake of all the world's children one can hope that it continues.

FAMILY AND THE FUTURE

When conservatives deplore the decline of "family values," they mean their own version of what a family ought to be: male-headed, male-controlled, a man ruling his wife and children with God-given authority. Such a family might have been decreed by the Biblical God, but it was never decreed by nature.

Like whales, dolphins, elephants, and other intelligent mammals, humans originally formed their clans and tribes around the matrilineal blood bond, with important lines of descent passing through the females. Offspring tended to stay close to their mothers for life. Robert Briffault says: "The maternal totemic clan was by far the most successful form that human association has assumed–it may indeed be said that it has been the only successful one... Social humanity has never succeeded in adequately replacing this primitive bond to which it owes its existence."[1]

Mythological traditions and early artifacts show that during the Stone Ages, only mothers were recognized as true parents. The oldest known clan names were those of ancestresses. Men had no part in transmitting the blood bond of kinship. They belonged to their mothers' clans. The extended family was held together by women.[2]

To some degree this is still true. Where extended families exist, it is largely the women who maintain bonds between family members. The support group provided by the extended family, living in village-like physical proximity, is far and away the best means of developing good citizens and well-adjusted individuals. Today, families are often fragmented by economic necessities, or divorce, or relocation, or simply by residence in a highly urbanized environment. To claim parental authority for men, patriarchal societies have tried many modifications, but most have had significant faults.

In medieval Europe, the church served as a model for patriarchal organizations everywhere, and sought always to denigrate the natural authority of mothers, to break up the old pagan-based matrifocal family whenever possible. Up to the eleventh century, Catholic priests were allowed to marry, until it became evident that family life diverted their attention; and most importantly, it diverted their money and property from the church. They willed assets to their children instead of to God. Therefore, a series of papal decretals commanded married clergymen to turn their wives out of their homes, sell their children as slaves, and disinherit their family members in favor of the church.[3]

This new rule was supported by the extreme hostility toward marriage in the writings of the early Christian fathers, and by Jesus's own insistence that no man could be his disciple unless he would renounce and "hate" his own parents, wife, and children (Luke 14:26).

Christian churches now pretend to have supported "family values" throughout history, but were actually opposed to marriage and the family for a long time. Early Christians' insistence on celibacy, virginity, the sinfulness of sex and the undesirability of motherhood weakened the family structure, to the enrichment of the church at the expense of the state. Christianity's gradual conquest of Europe consistently caused destruction of tribal laws of matrilineal inheritance, and ecclesiastical takeover of properties formerly controlled by women.[4]

To patriarchal thinkers, women and children were not so much interbonded individuals as living raw material for the political power base: breeders, workers, soldiers. Women in patriarchal marriages were (and still are) encouraged to produce many offspring, at any cost to their own health and comfort. Even today the anti-abortion and anti-birth control stance of religious fundamentalists shows a preference for quantity over quality of life, fostering many births of unwanted or unloved children destined to become wards of a state that can't care for them, and against which many will rebel in criminal ways. Even more reprehensible is the lack of birth control in a world whose entire future existence is severely threatened by a hugely dangerous problem of human overpopulation.

Though women especially yearn *not* to see their sons go off to war, to be maimed or killed, some of the most sexist thinkers have had the temerity to blame even the patriarchal phenomenon of war on women. The pejorative term "momism" was introduced by Philip Wylie in his *Generation of Vipers*, which actually claimed that the root cause of World War II and all other wars was the heartless greed of mothers, the "moms" who demanded that their sons fight wars to win them a more luxurious lifestyle.

The truth is that for centuries, older men have been luring or coercing sons away from their homes and sending them into battle, to increase the power of the Old Boys' Club, to kill off younger and more virile rivals, and to erode the power of women. War is a phenomenon of male-dominated societies, not of the ancient female-oriented ones that showed more respect for the living.

A truly humane civilization would have cultural taboos against war, as strong as our present taboos against cannibalizing the dead. It makes no sense to respect a dead body more than a live one. It makes even less sense to neglect that vital blood bond that mothers feel in their very cores; that is the basic family value that deserves much more consideration than the patriarchal idea of what family values are.

It must be said repeatedly, however, that hostility to patriarchal values does *not* mean pitting all women against all men. It is not a matter of individual against individual. Certainly many modern men embrace the pre-Christian vision of the family even if they are not specifically aware of it; they respect women, love their parents and their children, and try to keep peace in the world. And certainly many women have been brainwashed into a militant patriarchy.

Ignorant men sometimes put down modern feminism as a threat to family structures, claiming that feminist women will mistreat husbands and children. In reality, feminism strives for more emphasis on the family rather than less, with more general recognition of the vital central role of motherhood.

Patriarchal men express fear that women's acquisition of power will impel them to behave with the same abusive contempt that many men have used toward females. But women don't strive for the kinds of hierarchies that men like, with their authoritative tendencies to control with fear and violence. Women prefer consensus and voluntary cooperation, based on bonds of affection and personal responsibility. Like all female mammals, women are genetically programmed to care for creatures weaker than themselves. Left to follow natural inclinations, women tend to establish stable communities.

The real cause of decline of the family is patriarchal thinking, not feminism. When women cease to be respected for their creative nurturing behaviors, the family fails to uphold the society of which it is the primary root.

Today, with more than half of U.S. marriages ending in divorce, it's obvious that men and women need better training in how to get along with one another. Much of that training should actively reject former sexist attitudes that foster contempt for women. Men need to be taught to be good lovers, tolerant husbands, and kind fathers: in many ways, the exact opposite of the training given them in a culture of aggression, violence, and authoritarian conceit.

The human family is essential to the development of a humane civilization, and women are the foundation of the family. Let that be recognized, and we may be able to take a few steps out of the barbarism that patriarchy has foisted upon us.

Toward that end, let us IMAGINE.

Imagine a world in which no child is ever born unwanted or unloved, because every pregnancy carried to term is the result of conscious planning and preparation. Every baby comes into the world welcomed by the community, whose members may help the mother raise her child with gentle nurture and teaching.

Imagine a world where personal or collective violence is not considered a valid way of solving problems. Television and films don't glorify acts of violence; they are considered ugly. On the other hand, sensuality is considered highly entertaining and may be shown explicitly even to children, so they may grow up well trained to love.

Imagine a world in which there are no father-headed families or desperately striving single mothers, but cooperative groups who help each other raise children, care for the sick and aged, and do the work of the community, each according to his or her capabilities. Both men and women understand the need for good parenting, and every person honors his or her birthgiving mother for a lifetime. Biological fathers also receive respect if they play an active and useful part in the child's upbringing, but mere begetting is seen as less important than the complex biology of mothering.

Imagine a world in which people learn to help each other as naturally as, now, they learn to compete; a world where games are cooperative rather than aggressive; where common courtesy is extended to all without discrimination, and invidious comparisons are not made between one human function and another. For example, a trash collector or a farm laborer is recognized as being just as essential to the welfare of the community as a white-collar desk jockey, if not more so.

Imagine a world in which the sentient lives of animals are as much respected as the lives of humans, and no animal is ever willfully hurt or damaged. Killing of domestic animals for meat must be carried out in a quick, clean, painless manner, and no wild animals are hunted. People don't wear natural fur coats or ornaments of ivory and tortoiseshell, or any other product of wild animal slaughter. People are trained from infancy to care for their pets with competence and kindness, to make their lives happy and their deaths free from suffering.

Imagine a world in which people also are allowed to die without suffering, where the terminally ill may plan a painless suicide whenever they wish it. Doctors automatically provide pain-free lethal drugs to any terminally ill person of sound mind who requests them, and family members support the decision. Like birthgiving, dying is viewed as an individual choice, to be respected by others, who are obligated to provide help when needed.

Imagine a world in which people generally want for each other what mothers generally want for their children: a minimum of suffering and a maximum of enjoyment, with the satisfactions of being useful, and the fulfillment of love. Creativity and playfulness are encouraged; sound scientific education is universally provided; trust and helpfulness are maintained; and deliberately making someone unhappy is considered a primary sin.

Imagine a world where people are not greedy or envious, because everyone has enough to live comfortably, and no one has too much or too little. Acquisitiveness and conspicuous consumption are not admired, but rather viewed as bad manners. People work hard, but those who can't work–the sick, the elderly, and the very young–are supported.

Imagine a world in which there is no punitive, demanding God, but only a Goddess image representing the collective forces of nature, revered as a cultural symbol of human awe in the face of nature's intricacy and beauty. Such a Goddess is not in any sense transcendent, but immanent in the human spirit, especially the spirit of motherhood, and supportive of ongoing scientific investigation of her many mysteries.

Imagine a world in which there is peace on earth, and men's goodwill toward women. It was known long ago in some parts of this planet. Will it ever be known again?

As we seek routes toward a kinder, gentler future, the new feminism seems to be a hopeful signpost. In societies where women created most of the ethical and moral codes, people were usually more peaceable, contented, cooperative, and better supported by their kinship structures. Mothers' natural desire to promote the health and happiness of their children seems to have been reflected in the social rules formulated by matrifocal societies, whereas patriarchies like our own have engendered many oppressive restrictions aggressively imposed by violence or cruelty.

Any television viewer or moviegoer knows how much attention our culture gives to violent behavior patterns, including war, murder, assault, rape, and "heroic" shoot-em-ups. Media moguls like to say this is what the public demands; but human children, like apes, tend to imitate whatever they see, without passing it through any moral filter. When cruelty is the visual input, behavioral output may copy it.

Most women disprove the media moguls' contention by disliking the violence that masquerades as entertainment, just as most women disagree with the "he-man" contention that slaughtering wild animals is fun, or that real manhood should somehow involve physical abuse, either given or taken.

There are indications that women are beginning to get in touch with their own fundamental nature in ways that have been forbidden to them by their patriarchal culture. There is a fast-spreading tendency among women to reject remote, violent male deities with their crusades, witch hunts, inquisitions and battlefield invocations, now that the doleful history of religious sexism has made it clear that the God created in the image of man has promoted more cruelty than any other single cause.

The resurgence or rehabilitation of a Goddess image, to which men as well as women can relate in positive ways, may show the way to a wiser future, where human beings may finally live free of prejudice, exploitation, and violence; where women and children may safely walk any street, in any city, at any time of day or night; where no one suffers harassment or discrimination on the job or at home; where no child is born unwanted, unloved, or neglected. Mother Earth desperately needs more quality and less quantity of human life, and she needs it soon, or she may run out of all the things we need to sustain us: water, food, oil, minerals, and other resources.

Let us hope that, as one of her brainier species, we may have brains enough to bring about proper usage of ourselves and our resources, before we allow ourselves to destroy our home.

Notes

1. Briffault 2, 493-494.
2. Walker, W.E.M.S., 680-694.
3. Smith, 263; Boulding, 399.
4. Walker, W.E.M.S., 620-624.

RECOMMENDED READING

The following is a list of books that I have read (or written) over the years, and found especially enlightening. I trust that the reader will find it useful and may consult it in addition to the titles listed in the Bibliography.

BARBARA'S BOOK LIST

Abelard, Miles R. *Physicians of No Value: The Repressed Story of Ecclesiastical Flummery* (Reality Publications, 1979).

Acharya S. *The Christ Conspiracy: The Greatest Story Ever Sold* (Adventures Unlimited Press, 1999).

Acharya S. *Suns of God: Krishna, Buddha and Christ Unveiled* (Adventures Unlimited Press, 2004).

Armstrong, Karen. *A History of God* (Random House Publishing Group, 2011).

Armstrong, Karen. *The Battle for God: A History of Fundamentalism* (Random House Publishing Group, 2011).

Arnheim, Michael. *Is Christianity True?* (Duckworth, 1984).

Barnes, Julian. *Nothing to be Frightened Of* (Random House of Canada, 2010).

Barker, Dan. *Losing Faith in Faith: From Preacher to Atheist* (FFRF, Inc. 1992).

Barker, Dan. *Godless* (Ulysses Press, 2008).

Blaker, Kimberly (ed.) *The Fundamentals of Extremism: the Christian Right in America* (New Boston Books, 2003).

Bloom, Harold. *The American Religion* (Chu Hartley Publishers, 2006).

Campbell, Joseph. *The Masks of God: Primitive Mythology* (Volumes 1-4) (Viking Press, 1969).

Campbell, Joseph. *The Hero with a Thousand Faces* (New World Library, 2008).
Campbell, Joseph. *The Mythic Image* (Princeton University Press, 1981).
Carroll, James. *Constantine's Sword: The Church and the Jews* (Houghton Mifflin Harcourt, 2002).
Cranston, Sylvia, ed. *Reincarnation: The Phoenix Fire Mystery* (Theosophical University Press, 1998).
Daly, Mary. *Beyond God the Father: Toward a Philosophy of Women's Liberation* (Beacon Press, 1985).
Daly, Mar. *Gyn/ecology: The Metaethics of Radical Feminism* (Beacon Press, 1990).
Darwish, Nonie. *Cruel and Usual Punishment: The Terrifying Global Implications of Islamic Law* (Thomas Nelson, 2009).
Dawkins, Richard. *The God Delusion* (Houghton Mifflin Harcourt, 2008).
Dawkins, Richard. *A Devil's Chaplain* (Houghton Mifflin Harcourt, 2004).
De Meo, James. *Saharasia: The 4000 BCE Origins of Child Abuse, Sex-repression, Warfare and Social Violence in the Deserts of the Old World* (Orgone Biophysical Research Lab, 1998).
Dennet, Daniel C. *Breaking the Spell* (Penguin, 2006).
De Rosa, Peter. *Vicars of Christ: The Dark Side of the Papacy* (Poolbeg Press, 2000).
Doane, T.W. *Bible Myths and Their Parallels in Other Religions* (Truth Seeker Company, 1882).
Doherty, Earl. *The Jesus Puzzle: Did Christianity Begin with a Mythical Christ?* (Age of Reason Publications, 2005).
Ellerbe, Helen. *The Dark Side of Christian History* (Morningstar Books, 1995).
Fitzgerald, David. *Nailed: Ten Christian Myths That Show Jesus Never Existed at All* (Lulu, 2010).
Flew, Antony. *God: A Critical Enquiry* (Open Court Publishing Co., 1984)
Fox, Robin Lane. *The Unauthorized Version: Truth and Fiction in the Bible* (Penguin Books, 2006).

Frazer, Sir James. *The Golden Bough* (The Floating Press, 2009).
Freke, Timothy, & Gandy, Peter. *The Jesus Mysteries* (Crown Publishing Group, 2001).
Gabriel, Brigitte. *Because They Hate* (Macmillan, 2008).
Galanter, Marc. *Cults: Faith, Healing and Coercion* (Oxford University Press, 1999).
Gaylor, Annie Laurie (ed.). *Women Without Superstition* (Freedom From Religion Foundation, 1997).
Graham, Lloyd M. *Deceptions and Myths of the Bible* (Skyhorse Publishing Inc., 2012)
Greeley, Roger E. *Best of Robert Ingersoll* (Prometheus Books, 1983).
Green, Ruth Hurmence. *The Born Again Skeptic's Guide to the Bible* (Truman Green, 1992).
Harpur, Tom. *The Pagan Christ: Recovering the Lost Light* (Walker, 1995).
Harris, Sam. *The End of Faith* (W. W. Norton & Company, 2005).
Harris, Sam. *Letter to a Christian Nation* (Knopf, 2006).
Hayes, Judith. *The Happy Heretic* (Prometheus Books, 2000).
Hedges, Chris. *American Fascists: The Christian Right and the War on America* (Simon and Schuster, 2008).
Hirsi Ali, Ayaan. *Infidel* (Simon and Schuster, 2008).
Hitchens, Christopher. *God is Not Great* (Atlantic Books, 2011).
Holden, Andrew. *Jehovah's Witnesses* (Routledge, 2012).
Hosseini, Khaled. *A Thousand Splendid Suns* (Penguin, 2008).
Haught, James A. *2000 Years of Disbelief: Famous People with the Courage to Doubt* (Prometheus, 1996).
Ingersoll, Robert. *About the Holy Bible* (C. P. Farrell, 1894).
Jacoby, Susan. *Freethinkers: A History of American Secularism* (Macmillan, 2005).
Jessop, Carolyn. *Escape* (Crown Publishing Group, 2007).
Johnson, Chalmers. *Nemesis: The Last Days of the American Republic* (Macmillan, 2007).
Kennedy, Eugene. *The Unhealed Wound: The Church, the Priesthood, and the Question of Sexuality* (Macmillan, 2002).
Kimball, Charles. *When Religion Becomes Evil* (HarperCollins, 2002).

Kristof, Nicholas and WuDunn, Sheryl. *Half the Sky* (Knopf Doubleday Publishing Group, 2009).
Kurtz, Paul. *The Transcendental Temptation* (Prometheus, 2013).
Lamont, Corliss. *The Illusion of Immortality* (G. P. Putnam's Sons, 2011).
Lea, Henry Charles. *A History of the Inquisition of the Middle Ages* (Volumes 1-3) (Harper & Brothers, 1888).
Leedom, Tim C. (Ed.). *The Book Your Church Doesn't Want You to Read* (Truth Seeker Co., 1993).
Martin, Walter. *The Kingdom of the Cults* (Baker Books, 2003).
McCabe, Joseph. *The Myth of the Resurrection* (Haldeman-Julius Company, 1925).
Muller, Herbert J. *The Uses of the Past* (Schocken Books, 1985).
Newton, Michael. *Holy Homicide* (Loompanics Unlimited, 1998).
Onfray, Michael. *Atheist Manifesto* (Skyrose Publishing, 2013).
Pagels, Elaine. *The Gnostic Gospels* (Random House Publishing, 2004).
Phillips, Kevin. *American Theocracy* (Penguin Books, 2006).
Pigliucci, Massimo. *Denying Evolution: Creationism, Scientism, and the Nature of Science* (W.H. Freeman, 2002).
Pinker, Steven. *The Blank Slate: The Modern Denial of Human Nature* (Penguin, 2003).
Ranke-Heinemann, Uta. *Eunuchs for the Kingdom of Heaven* (Penguin Books, 1991).
Robertson, J. M. *Pagan Christs: Studies in Comparative Hierology* (Watts, 1903).
Rudin, Arnold James. *The Baptizing of America: The Religious Right's Plan for the Rest of Us* (Thunder's Mouth Press, 2006).
Sagan, Carl. *The Demon-Haunted World* (Random House Publishing Group, 2011).
Schell, Jonathan. *The Fate of the Earth* (Stanford University Press, 2000).
Shelley, Percy Bysshe. *The Necessity of Atheism* (Prometheus Books, 2010).
Shermer, Michael. *Why People Believe Weird Things* (Macmillan, 2002).

Smith, George H. *Atheism: The Case Against God* (Prometheus, 2010).
Smith, Homer. *Man and His Gods.* (Grosset & Dunlap, 1971).
Smith, Warren Allen. *Who's Who in Hell* (Barricade Books, 2000).
Spong, John Shelby. *Why Christianity Must Change or Die* (HarperCollins, 2009).
Stone, Merlin. *When God Was a Woman* (Knopf Doubleday Publishing Group, 2012).
Thomas, Keith. *Religion and the Decline of Magic* (Penguin UK, 2003).
Walker, Barbara G. *Man Made God* (Stellar House Publishing, 2010).
Walker, Barbara G. *The Woman's Encyclopedia of Myths and Secrets* (Castle Books, 1996).
Walker, Barbara G. *The Woman's Dictionary of Symbols and Sacred Objects* (HarperCollins, 1998).
Walker, Barbara G. *The Crone: Woman of Age, Wisdom, and Power* (HarperCollins, 2013).
Walker, Barbara G. *The Skeptical Feminist* (Harper & Row, 1987).
Warraq, Ibn. *Why I Am Not a Muslim* (Prometheus Books, 1995).
Wheless, Joseph. *Forgery in Christianity* (Cosmo, Inc. 2007).
White, Andrew D. *A History of the Warfare of Science with Theology in Christendom* (Cosimo, Inc. 2010).
Yallop, David A. *In God's Name* (Constable & Robinson, 2012).

BIBLIOGRAPHY

Abelard, Miles R. *Physicians of No Value* (Winter Park, FL: Reality Publications, 1979)

Attwater, Donald. *The Penguin Dictionary of Saints* (Baltimore, MD: Penguin Books, 1965).

Bering, Jesse. *The Belief Instinct*. (New York: Norton, 2011).

Blaker, Kimberly (ed.) *The Fundamentals of Extremism: The Christian Right in America* (New Boston, MI: New Boston Books, 2003).

Boulding, Elise. *The Underside of History* (Boulder, CO: Westview Press, 1976).

Branston, Brian. *The Lost Gods of England* (London: Thames & Hudson, 1957).

Briffault, Robert. *The Mothers* (Volumes 1-3) (New York: Macmillan, 1927).

Budge, E.A. Wallis. *The Gods of the Egyptians* (Volumes 1-2) (New York: Dover, 1964).

Bufe, Charles (ed.) *The Heretic's Handbook of Quotations* (Tucson, AZ: Sharp Press, 1998).

Bullough, Vern L., Shelton, Brenda, and Slavin, Sarah. *The Subordinated Sex*. (Chicago, IL: Dell, 1974)

Campbell, Joseph. *The Masks of God: Occidental Mythology* (New York: Viking Press, 1964).

Campbell, Joseph. *The Masks of God: Creative Mythology* (New York: Viking Press, 1968).

Campbell, Joseph. *The Mythic Image* (Princeton, NJ: Princeton University Press, 1974).

Condren, Mary. *The Serpent and the Goddess: Women, Religion, and Power in Celtic Ireland* (San Francisco: Harper & Row, 1989).

Cranston, Sylvia, ed. *Reincarnation: The Phoenix Fire Mystery* (Theosophical University Press, 1998).

Darwish, Nonie. *Cruel and Usual Punishment* (Thomas Nelson, 2008).
Davidson, Terry. *Conjugal Crime* (New York: Hawthorn Books Inc., 1978).
Dawkins, Richard. *The God Delusion* (New York: Houghton Mifflin Harcourt, 2008).
DeMeo, James. *Saharasia: The 4000 BCE Origins of Child Abuse, Sex-repression, Warfare and Social Violence in the Deserts of the Old World* (Greensprings, OR: Orgone Research Lab, 1998).
Dennet, Daniel C. *Breaking the Spell: Religion as a Natural Phenomenon* (New York: Viking Press, 2006).
de Riencourt, A. *Sex and Power in History* (NY: Dell, 1974).
Dumezil, Georges. *Archaic Roman Religion* (Chicago, IL: University of Chicago Press, 1970).
Eisenach, Emlyn. *Husbands, Wives, and Concubines* (Kirksville, MO: Truman State University Press, 2004).
Evans, Bergen. *The Natural History of Nonsense* (New York: Alfred A. Knopf, 1965).
Evans, Rod L. and Berent, Irwin N. *Fundamentalism: Hazards and Heartbreaks* (LaSalle, IL: Open Court, 1988).
Fielding, William J. Strange *Customs of Courtship and Marriage* (New York: Garden City Publishing Co., 1942).
Freke, Timothy, and Gandy, Peter. *Jesus and the Lost Goddess* (New York: Three Rivers Press, 2001).
Freke, Timothy, and Gandy, Peter. *The Jesus Mysteries* (New York: Harmony Books, 1999).
Gabriel, Brigitte. *Because They Hate* (New York: St. Martin's Press, 2006).
Gaylor, Annie Laurie (ed.) *Women Without Superstition* (Madison, WI: FFRF, Inc., 1997).
Gifford, Edward S., Jr. *The Evil Eye* (New York: Macmillan, 1958).
Graham, Lloyd M. *Deceptions and Myths of the Bible* (Carol Publishing Group, 1999).
Graves, Robert. *The Greek Myths* (Volumes 1-2) (New York: Penguin Books Inc., 1955).

Harris, Sam. *The End of Faith: Religion, Terror, and the Future of Reason* (New York: W.W. Norton, 2005).
Haught, James A. *2000 Years of Disbelief: Famous People with the Courage to Doubt* (Prometheus, 1996).
Hazlitt, W. Carew. *Faiths and Folklore of the British Isles* (New York: Random House, 1979).
Hedges, Chris. *Empire of Illusion* (Nation Books, 2009).
Hooke, S.H. *Middle Eastern Mythology* (Harmondsworth, England: Penguin Books Ltd., 1963).
Konner, Joan (ed.) *The Atheist's Bible* (New York: HarperCollins, 2007).
Kramer, Heinrich, and Sprenger, James. *Malleus Maleficarum* (New York: Dover, 1971).
Langley, Roger, and Levy, Richard C. *Wife Beating: The Silent Crisis* (New York: E.P. Dutton & Co., 1977).
Lash, John. *Not in His Image: Gnostic Vision, Sacred Ecology, and the Future of Belief* (Chelsea Green, 2006).
Lea, Henry Charles. *The Inquisition of the Middle Ages* (New York: Macmillan, 1961).
Lederer, Wolfgang. *The Fear of Women* (New York: Harcourt Brace Jovanovich, 1968).
Legman, G. *Rationale of the Dirty Joke* (New York: Grove Press, 1968).
Malvern, Marjorie. *Venus in Sackcloth* (Carbondale, IL: Southern Illinois University Press, 1975).
Miles, Clement A. *Christmas Customs and Traditions* (New York: Dover Publications, 1976).
Mills, David. *Atheist Universe: The Thinking Person's Answer to Christian Fundamentalism* (Berkeley, CA: Ulysses Press, 2006).
Morris, Joan. *The Lady Was a Bishop* (New York: Macmillan, 1973).
Muller, Herbert J. *The Uses of the Past* (New York: New American Library, 1954).
Nafisi, Azar. *Reading Lolita in Tehran* (New York: Random House, 2003).

Neumann, Erich. *Amor and Psyche* (New York: Harper & Row, 1958).
Neumann, Erich. *The Great Mother: An Analysis of the Archetype* (Princeton, NJ: Princeton Univ. Press, 1963).
Noble, David F. *A World Without Women* (New York: Knopf, 1992).
O'Flaherty, Wendy Doniger. *Hindu Myths* (Harmondsworth, England: Penguin Books Ltd., 1975).
Onfray, Michael. *Atheist Manifesto* (New York: Arcade Publishing, 2005).
Pagels, Elaine. *The Gnostic Gospels* (New York: Random House, 1979).
Pinker, Steven. *The Better Angels of Our Nature* (New York: Viking Penguin, 2011).
Ranke-Heinemann, Uta. *Eunuchs for the Kingdom of Heaven* (New York: Doubleday, 1990).
Rawson, Philip. *Erotic Art of the East* (New York: G.P. Putnam's Sons, 1968).
Rawson, Philip. *The Art of Tantra* (Greenwich, CT: New York Graphic Society, 1973).
Robbins, Rossell Hope. *The Encyclopedia of Witchcraft and Demonology* (New York: Crown Publishers, 1959).
Ruthven, Malise. *The Divine Supermarket: Shopping for God in America* (New York: William Morrow, 1989).
Sagan, Carl. *The Demon-Haunted World* (New York: Random House, 1995).
Smith, Homer. *Man and His Gods* (Boston: Little, Brown, 1952).
Spong, John Shelby. *Why Christianity Must Change or Die* (HarperSanFrancisco, 1998).
Spretnak, Charlene (ed.). *The Politics of Women's Spirituality* (Garden City, NY: Anchor/Doubleday, 1982).
Stanton, Elizabeth Cady. *The Original Feminist Attack on the Bible* (NY: Arno Press, 1974).
Stein, Gordon. *The Encyclopedia of Unbelief* (Buffalo, NY: Prometheus Books, 1985).

Sullivan, Francis A. *The Church We Believe in: One, Holy, Catholic, and Apostolic* (New York: Paulist Press, 1988).
Turville-Petre, E. O. G. *Myth and Religion of the North* (New York: Holt, Rinehart & Winston, 1964).
Walker, Barbara G. *Man Made God* (Seattle, WA: Stellar House Publishing, 2010).
Walker, Barbara G. *The Woman's Encyclopedia of Myths and Secrets* (HarperSanFrancisco, 1983).
Warraq, Ibn. *Why I Am Not a Muslim* (Amherst, New York: Prometheus, 1995).
Wedeck, Harry E. *A Treasury of Witchcraft* (Secaucus, NJ: Citadel Press, 1975).
Wolf, Naomi. *The Beauty Myth: How Images of Beauty are Used Against Women* (New York: William Morrow, 1991).

ABOUT THE AUTHOR

Barbara G. Walker is a researcher, lecturer, and author of 24 books and numerous articles on comparative religion, history, mythology, symbolism, mineral lore, the Tarot, the *I Ching*, a collection of original "Feminist Fairy Tales," an autobiography, a novel, and her latest, *Man Made God*. Her *Woman's Encyclopedia of Myths and Secrets* has been continuously in print since 1983 and was named Book of the Year by the London Times. She has received the Humanist Heroine of the Year award from the American Humanist Association, the Women Making Herstory award from New Jersey NOW, and the Olympia Brown award from the Unitarian Universalist Association. She is also listed in that prestigious publication, *Who's Who in Hell*.

As an artist, she created 78 original paintings for the Barbara Walker Tarot Deck, and 64 more for her *I Ching* of the Goddess card deck, both published with companion books. She has also worked as a professional knitwear designer, and her books on knitting patterns are American classics. She personally invented more than a thousand original pattern stitches, more than any other single person known to history, and created a new technique that she named Mosaic Knitting.

A Phi Beta Kappa graduate of the University of Pennsylvania, she has worked as a journalist, dance teacher, painter, designer, workshop leader, and mentor of women's spirituality groups as well as a wife and mother, and has presented many talks for Humanist, Unitarian, and Freethinker organizations.

www.ingramcontent.com/pod-product-compliance
Lightning Source LLC
Chambersburg PA
CBHW071711090426
42738CB00009B/1743